CLASSIC
SOUTHWEST
Cooking

Classic Southwest Recipes
Authentic Family Favorites

Sheryn R. Jones
Cookbook Resources, LLC

Classic Southwest Cooking

1st Printing   July 2004

2nd Printing September 2005

Copyright © 2004

By Sheryn R. Jones, Highland Village, Texas. All rights reserved.

ISBN: 1-931294-65-8

Library of Congress Number: 2004109683

Edited, Designed and Published in the
United States of America by
Cookbook Resources, LLC
541 Doubletree Drive
Highland Village, Texas 75077
Toll free 866-229-2665
www.cookbookresources.com
Manufactured in China

Bringing Family And Friends To The Table

Introduction

The goal of *Classic Southwest Cooking* is to capture the home cooking enjoyed by families in the Southwest and to preserve this unique, regional home cooking in a practical, entertaining cookbook.

Most of the recipes are simple because Southwest cooking is simple. Most of the recipes are enjoyed by families and friends and are part of everyday life. The occasional time-consuming recipes, tamales for instance, are included to give you a complete feel for Southwest cooking rather than encourage you to spend all day in the kitchen. It is a lot easier and just as good to buy tamales from Hispanics who have been making them all their lives.

The second goal of *Classic Southwest Cooking* is to present a cookbook that is entertaining to read. You don't have to cook to enjoy this cookbook. You can take an imaginary trip to the Southwest and vicariously experience other traditions, another culture and regional foods. Besides, you'll cook something from this cookbook one day.

And the third goal of this cookbook is to convey some sense for the extraordinary history and tradition that is the foundation for this very unique, regional cuisine. No other regional cuisine in the U.S. has the long history that Southwest cooking has. No other regional cuisine is the direct descendent of the original peoples who lived on the lands as far back as 1000 AD. Southwest cooking demands that its history be a part of it. And Southwest cooking earns our respect for its development, its continuation and for its traditions.

By understanding how and why regional foods develop, we better understand the lifestyles of people who are our neighbors. We broaden our views and appreciation for traditions and old cultures and in doing so, strengthen our own families and our own little piece of the world.

Thank you for reading this cookbook and for taking an interest in one of the most extraordinary regional cuisines in the world.

Sheryn R. Jones
Editor

TABLE OF

CONTENTS

Southwest Foods

Southwest cooking is a glorious mix of Native American Indian, Mexican and Anglo-American foods and traditions. No other regional cuisine has such meager beginnings and has grown to such world acclaim.

To fully appreciate Southwest cooking, one must understand its basic ingredients and look to its history for the evolution of a fascinating and superbly flavorful cuisine.

The staples of the Aztec Indians who roamed Mexico were chile peppers, beans, corn and squash. Spanish explorers brought these foods north and resident Indians used them with their native foods as well as those brought by English-speaking people.

Pinon nuts, nopalitos, cilantro, avocados, spotted pinto beans, black beans, garbanzo beans and masa harina became integral ingredients in Southwest cooking.

From these first ingredients to present-day, the most distinguishing ingredient in Southwest cooking is the chile pepper. Primary dishes that include chiles are Basic Red Sauce, Basic Green Chile Sauce, Ranchero Sauce, Taco Sauce, Hot Sauce and Roasted Chile Salsa, Red Chile Stews, Carne Avocado, Enchiladas, Tamales, Tortillas and dozens more.

No other vegetable has had a greater effect on a way of life and a way of cooking than the chiles of the Southwest have had. For more than 500 years Southwest cooking remains one of the most colorful and exciting regional cuisines in the U.S.

★ This symbol to the left of recipe names identifies classic Southwest dishes.

All About Chiles

FRESH CHILE PEPPERS

New Mexico Green Chiles are the predominant chile peppers used in Southwest cooking. These long, green chiles are about 6 to 7 inches long with about a 1½ to 2-inch shoulder and taper to a rounded point. They are mild to hot and vary with the season. The best flavor comes from roasting and removing the outside skin. They may be eaten raw, roasted, dried, canned, whole or stuffed. They have a distinctive chile flavor that is earthy and crisp. They are used in salsas, soups, stews, casseroles, salads and sauces. They are an essential ingredient in basic red and green chile sauces. When they are ripe, they turn red and may be dried. They are called **New Mexico red chile**s in the dried form. The best known agricultural region for growing chiles is in and around Hatch, New Mexico, in the southern part of the state.

Anaheim Green Chiles are about 5 to 6 inches long and have a tapered tip. They are usually green, but sometimes red and are relatively mild. They may be used as a substitute for the New Mexico green chile when it is not available. Anaheim chiles are sometimes mistaken for New Mexico chiles, but they are a different variety of the New Mexico chile. They are sometimes called the California green chile. They are used much the same way that New Mexico green chiles are used.

Jalapenos are about 2 to 3 inches long with a tapered end and about a 1 inch shoulder (the part under the stem). They are deep green or red, sometimes with tan or brown stripes. Jalapenos have a mild to hot flavor and are the most popular pepper in the U.S. They are used in salsas, sauces, dips, stews, chile, bread, pickled and stuffed. The dried form is called **chipotle**.

Poblano peppers are about 5 to 6 inches long, about 2 to 3 inches at the shoulder and more rounded than elongated. They are dark green and ripen to reddish-brown. They have a mild flavor and are best when roasted and stuffed for rellenos or rajas. They are also used in soups, stews, sauces and salsas. The dried form is called **ancho**.

Serranos are small peppers about 2 to 2½ inches long and about ½ inch wide. They are bright green and turn scarlet red when ripe. They are very hot and care should be used when handling them. They are used in salsas, sauces and may be roasted. The dried form is called **chile seco**.

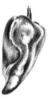

Habaneros are considered by some to be the hottest pepper in the world. They are closely related to Scotch bonnets and are small round peppers that may be dark green, orange or red. The habanero is estimated to be as much as 50 times hotter than jalapenos. Extreme caution should be used when handling these peppers and rubber gloves should be used at all times. Habaneros are used in salsas, chutneys and may be pickled.

DRIED CHILE PEPPERS

New Mexico Reds are also called chile colorado (colorado means red in Spanish). They are the dried version of the New Mexico green chile. The chile is essential for some of the red chile sauces in Southwest cooking and has a wonderful earthy flavor with a crisp, mild heat. They are used in sauces, stews, soups, ground as 100% pure chile powder and crushed as red pepper flakes. They are also used in the traditional, decorative ristras.

Chipotle peppers are smoke-dried **jalapenos** and are excellent for sauces, salsas, pastas and soups. They have a smoky, sweet, full-flavored heat that is very satisfying and very popular. They are used in sauces, stews and salsas and are available dried and canned in red adobe sauce.

Ancho peppers are dried **poblanos** and are about 3½ to 5 inches long and about 3 inches wide. They are mild to slightly hot with a dark, reddish-brown color. They have a woody, fruit flavor with tones of licorice and coffee. They are used primarily in moles and sauces.

Chile seco or **Serrano seco** are dried **Serrano chiles** and are hot. They measure about 1 to 2 inches long and about ½ inch wide and are orange in color. Their intense heat has a citrus flavor to it. They are used primarily in sauces and ground as a powder.

SCOVILLE HEAT RATINGS

The Scoville standard is a method of measuring the heat in various chiles and assigning a value or units of measure to the amount of capsaicin found in chiles. Listed below are standard ratings for chiles used in this cookbook.

Bell peppers	0 Scoville units
New Mexico Red	500 to 1,000 Scoville units
Poblano	1,000 to 1,500 Scoville units
Ancho (Dried Poblano)	1,000 to 1,500 Scoville units
Jalapeno	2,500 to 5,000 Scoville units
Chipotle (Dried Jalapeno)	2,500 to 5,000 Scoville units
Serrano	10,000 to 23,000 Scoville units
Habanero	100,000 to 300,000 Scoville units

ROASTING CHILE PEPPERS

To roast chiles, hold them over an open-flame gas burner with long metal fork or broil them in oven until outside turns dark brown on all sides. (Be careful not to burn holes through skin.) Place chiles in plastic bag, seal and allow to sweat for about 15 to 20 minutes so skin will slide off easily. Remove skins and slice through length of chile on one side. Remove seeds, but leave veins intact.

Roasting chiles may be done in one of 3 ways.
1. Over an open flame
2. Under the broiler in the oven
3. Baked in the oven

The outside skin should be browned or charred so that the skin begins to pull away from the flesh. After the chiles sweat sealed in a plastic bag or placed under a damp towel stretched over the baking pan, the skin slips off easily. Care should be taken not to break or burn holes in the flesh.

TOASTING DRIED CHILES

Place dried chiles on baking pan and bake in oven at 250° until chiles are lightly toasted, but not burned. Remove stems and seeds and grind in food proceessor. Store in an airtight container.

DRYING CHILES

Drying chiles is an easy way to keep them for use during the winter months to season soups, stews and sauces. When considering which chiles to dry, remember that the thinner the flesh of the chile, the quicker and better it will dry. The thicker flesh of a jalapeno, for instance, does not dry as well as thinner flesh chiles like the New Mexico Red.

To dry chiles, string and hang them in the sun for several days if you live in a dry area. If not, lay chiles on a cookie sheet and bake them at 200° for 5 to 6 hours or until they are adequately dry. Store them in an airtight container.

USING DRIED CHILES

A great way to use dried chiles is to grind them into various forms to use as seasonings. Chiles may be ground into flakes or into a fine powder, both with excellent results and usually better flavors than commercially prepared ground seasonings.

Another way to use dried chiles is to reconstitute or rehydrate dried chiles by soaking them in hot water for about 30 minutes or by rehydrating them in the sauce, soup or stew they season.

Gringo Glossary for Southwest Cooking

Albondigas – Spanish for meatballs; traditional Southwest dish with spicy meatballs in tomato sauce; also see Sopa de Albondigas

Anaheim Chile – A variety of the New Mexico green chile; sometimes more available than the New Mexico green or red chile; about 4 to 5 inches long with a pointed tip; Scoville rating 1,000 to 1,500

Ancho – Dried, mild poblano chile; Scoville rating 1,000 to 1,500

Antojitos – Spanish for appetizers

Arroz – Spanish for rice

Arroz Con Pollo – Spanish for rice with chicken

Asadero Cheese – White Mexican cheese similar to mozzarella; used primarily for melting; has rich buttery flavor; usually packaged into balls

Bizcochitos – Cookies with anise flavoring

Botanas – Spanish for drinks

Bowl of Red – Chili; meat dish with no beans

Bunelos – Deep-fried Mexican pastry sprinkled with sugar and cinnamon

Burrito – Warmed soft flour tortilla with a filling and wrapped like an envelope

Calabaza; Calabacitas – Type of squash used similarly to acorn and butternut squash; one of the staples of Southwest cooking

Caldo; Caldillo – Spanish for soup

Carne – Spanish for meat

Carne Adovada – Traditional Southwest dish of pork marinated in red chile sauce

Carne Asada – Traditional Southwest dish of grilled, marinated steak

Chihuahua Cheese – Mexican cheese similar to cheddar; melts well, but becomes stringy

Chile; Chiles – Peppers used in Southwest cooking; in New Mexico the plant and the dish are spelled with an "e"; spellings differ by region

Chile Con Queso – Traditional Mexican dip of melted cheese and green chiles; served with chips

Chile Molido – Pure ground red chile powder

Chile Peppers – The primary ingredient in Southwest cooking; see New Mexico green, red, jalapeno, serrano, poblano, ancho, chipotle, chile seco

Chile Seco – Dried serrano pepper; – Scoville rating 10,000 to 23,000

Chile Relleno – Green chile stuffed with cheese filling and deep-fried

Chili – Meat dish with no beans; New Mexico spelling is with "e"

Chimichanga – Tortilla with a filling, wrapped like an envelope and deep-fried

Chipotle chiles – Dried jalapeno chiles

Chorizo – Highly seasoned Mexican sausage

Cilantro – Leaves of coriander plant; same as Mexican parsley

Comino – Cumin; aromatic seed used as flavoring

Coriander – Plant from which cilantro grows; has round, pale yellow to brown seeds –

Enchilada – Tortilla with filling, rolled into log shape and chile sauces and cheese poured on top

Escabeche – Spanish for pickled in a marinade or vinegar

Flauta – Tortilla with filling, rolled very tightly and deep-fried

Frijoles – Pinto beans

Garbanzo Beans – Also called chickpeas; used in many Mexican and Southwest dishes including soups, stews, salads and dips; high in protein and low in fat

Hominy – Corn used to make grits, corn flakes, corn syrup, cornstarch and corn oil

Jalapeno Chiles – Jalapenos are about 2 to 3 inches long with a tapered end and about a 1-inch shoulder; usually green or red, sometimes with tan stripes; Scoville rating 2,500 to 5,000

Jicama – Large root vegetable with gray-brown skin; flavor is similar to radish and texture is similar to water chestnut; usually served raw in salads or salsas

Marinades – Seasonings and ingredients used to tenderize tough cuts of meat

Masa – Fresh corn dough

Masa harina – Dried and ground corn flour

Monterey Jack Cheese – Cheese used frequently in Southwest dishes; white, semi-soft cheese

Nachos – Tortilla chips covered with melted cheese, tomatoes, chiles, beans, guacamole, sour cream

New Mexico Green Chile Essential ingredient in many Southwest dishes using chiles; basic ingredient in red chile sauces; earthy flavor with crisp, mild heat; Scoville rating 500 to 1,000; Anaheim chile is a variety of New Mexico chiles and may be used as a substitute

New Mexico Red Chile – Dried New Mexico green chile; also called chile colorado; essential ingredient in many Southwest dishes using chiles; basic ingredient in red chile sauces; earthy flavor with crisp, mild heat; Scoville rating 500 to 1,000

Nopalitos – Prepared pads of the prickly pear cactus

Picante – Hot, highly seasoned

Poblano Chile – Mild chiles about 4 to 5 inches long, several inches wide at the shoulder and rounded instead of elongated; dark green and ripen to reddish-brown; Scoville rating 1,000 to 1,500

Quesadilla – Tortilla filled with cheese, meat and/or salsa, folded in half and heated until cheese melts

Queso Fresca – Mexican cheese similar to farmers cheese; feta cheese may be substituted

Refritos – Refried beans

Ristra – Decorative wreath or string of dried chiles used as accent

Salsa – Mixture of vegetables, fruits or nuts used to fill tortillas and to accompany Mexican dishes

Salsa Cruda – Fresh tomato salsa with tomatoes, onion, jalapenos, serranos, cilantro and garlic

Salsa Verde – Fresh tomatillos, cilantro and jalapenos finely diced and served in bowl with chips

Scoville Scale – Measurement of units of heat found in chile peppers; named after the man who invented it

Serrano Chile – Hot chile pepper about 1 to 1½ inches long, usually red, sometimes green or yellow; Scoville rating 10,000 to 23,000

Sopa – Spanish for soup

Sopa de Albondigas – Soup with spicy meatballs in a beef broth

Sopaipillas – Favorite sweet; triangles of flour, sugar and baking powder deep-fried and served hot with honey and powdered sugar

Taco – Soft or crispy tortilla filled with meat, cheese, tomatoes, onions and salsa

Tamale – Shredded pork in masa and wrapped in corn husks

Taquitas – Rolled, deep-fried tacos

Tex-Mex – Regional cuisine developed in Texas; should not be confused with Southwest regional cooking

Tomatillo – Mexican green tomato covered with papery husk; used raw in salsas and cooked in variety of Southwest dishes

Tortilla – Flat bread made from corn or flour and used in Mexican cooking

Tortilleria – A tortilla factory

Tostada – Tortilla that is flat or basket-shape and fried crisp

*Southwest Seasoning Mix

3 tablespoons ground red chiles
2 tablespoons paprika
1 tablespoon ground coriander
1 tablespoon dried parsley, crushed
1 tablespoon ground cumin
1 teaspoon salt
1 teaspoon dried oregano leaves, crushed
¼ teaspoon cayenne pepper
¾ teaspoon garlic powder

- Mix all ingredients well. Store in airtight container.

- Use this seasoning mix on vegetables, tossed salads, roast beef, grilled chicken, grilled seafood, pork, rice or pasta. Use sparingly.

*Red Chile Sauce

¼ cup olive oil
½ onion, minced
1 clove garlic, minced
2 tablespoons flour
⅓ cup chile powder
2 cups water
1 teaspoon oregano
½ teaspoon salt
½ teaspoon cumin

- Heat oil in skillet, add onion and garlic and cook until onion is translucent. Add flour, cook until bubbly and stir in chile powder, water, oregano, salt and cumin.

- Cook until sauce thickens, reduce heat and simmer about 5 minutes. Chill several hours before serving.

13

*Basic Red Chile Sauce

This basic red sauce is used in many Southwest dishes, including enchiladas, tacos and tamales. Traditionally, tomatoes are not used in red and green sauces. The traditional sauces focus on the flavors of the chiles.

8 to 10 large, dried New Mexican red chiles
3 cups water
3 to 4 cloves garlic, chopped
1 onion, chopped
1 teaspoon cumin

- Place dried chiles on baking pan and cook in oven at 250° until chiles are lightly toasted, but not burned. Remove stems and seeds. Crush or crumble chiles in water in saucepan.

- Add garlic, onion and cumin and bring to boil. Reduce heat and simmer for about 30 minutes. Pour water into blender and puree mixture until smooth.

- Pour into saucepan and heat until mixture reaches desired consistency. Sauce yields about 2 cups.

The primary dishes in Southwest cooking that use chile peppers include basic sauces used in huevos rancheros, red chile stews, carne adovado, enchiladas and tamales, in additional to other meat and vegetable dishes.

*Green Chile Sauce

Green chile sauce is used more commonly in southern New Mexico where the main agricultural crop is green chiles.

3 cloves garlic, chopped
1 large onion, chopped
2 tablespoons oil, divided
1 teaspoon cumin
1 teaspoon oregano
2 (14 ounce) cans chicken broth
8 to 10 New Mexico green chiles, roasted, peeled, seeded, chopped
1 tablespoon flour
Salt and pepper

- Heat 1 tablespoon oil in large skillet and saute garlic and onion until they are translucent. Add cumin and oregano. Pour in small amount of chicken broth and flour and stir until flour dissolves.

- Pour remaining broth and chiles in skillet and simmer for at least 30 minutes. Taste and adjust seasonings.

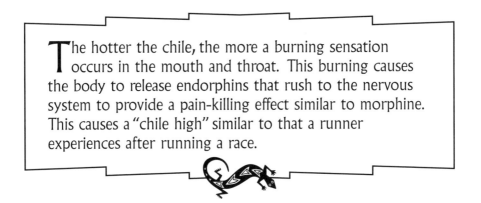

The hotter the chile, the more a burning sensation occurs in the mouth and throat. This burning causes the body to release endorphins that rush to the nervous system to provide a pain-killing effect similar to morphine. This causes a "chile high" similar to that a runner experiences after running a race.

✷Homemade Taco Sauce

This is a great sauce to have on hand in the refrigerator. Use on tacos, huevos ranchero, dips, breakfast burritos or any kind burrito.

1 (8 ounce) can tomato sauce
1 (4 ounce) can diced green chiles or 1 tablespoon sliced
    jalapeno peppers
3 cloves garlic, minced
3 green onions, minced
1 teaspoon cumin
1 teaspoon chile powder
1 teaspoon salt
½ teaspoon oregano
1 tablespoon fresh lemon juice
2 teaspoons vinegar

Mix all ingredients and store in refrigerator tightly covered.

Southwest cooking is a blend of traditional foods of the Anasazi-Pueblo tribes that includes blue corn, beans and squash and the green chiles and cooking techniques of the Aztec brought by the Spanish from Mexico City. This blend was furthered mixed with Anglo-American settlers beginning early in the 1800's until today, Southwest cooking is one of the most recognizable, regional cuisines in the world today.

*Basic Ranchero Sauce

Ranchero Sauce is well known in Huevos Ranchero and is used in many dishes with tomato-based sauce.

2 tablespoons (¼ stick) butter
2 onions, chopped
½ chopped celery
2 cloves garlic, minced
2 jalapeno peppers, seeded, chopped
1 tablespoon worcestershire sauce
1 (28 ounce) can chopped stewed tomatoes
½ teaspoon salt

Combine all ingredients in saucepan. Heat to boil, reduce heat and simmer for 1 hour or until sauce thickens.

*Quick Green Chile Sauce

1 (8 ounce) can tomato sauce
1 (4 ounce) can chopped green chiles
1 clove garlic, minced
½ onion, chopped
1 teaspoon crushed red pepper
Dash oregano
Salt

Mix all ingredients and store in refrigerator. Makes about 1 cup.

*New Mexico Hot Sauce

This green hot sauce is used more frequently than red hot sauce in the southern part of the Southwest.

½ cup cider vinegar
2 teaspoons sugar
2 teaspoons salt
4 to 6 New Mexico green chiles, roasted, peeled, seeded, minced

✋ Mix vinegar, sugar and salt well in medium bowl with lid. Add chiles and stir. Store covered in refrigerator for several weeks and stir before serving. Increase number of chiles to increase heat.

*Jalapeno Hot Sauce

¼ cup cider vinegar
1 teaspoons sugar
1 teaspoons salt
2 to 3 large jalapenos, seeded, minced

✋ Mix vinegar, sugar and salt well in medium bowl with lid. Add jalapenos and stir. Store covered in refrigerator for several weeks and stir before serving. Increase number of jalapenos to increase heat.

TIP: A wide variety of salsas are featured in the beginning of the Appetizer section.

APPETIZERS
&
BEVERAGES

*Real Homemade Salsa

3 large tomatoes, peeled, seeded, chopped
3 to 4 fresh New Mexico green chiles, roasted, seeded,
    minced
2 cloves garlic, minced
1 jalapeno chile, seeded, minced
1 bunch green onions with tops, minced
1 bunch fresh cilantro, snipped
½ teaspoon cumin
Salt and pepper

 Mix all ingredients in large bowl and chill several hours for flavors to blend. Serve in small bowls with chips or over fish or vegetables.

*Salsa Fresca

4 medium tomatoes, peeled, chopped
1 onion, minced
3 fresh jalapenos, minced
⅓ cup chopped fresh cilantro
1 clove garlic, minced
2 tablespoons lime juice
½ teaspoon salt
½ teaspoon pepper

 Combine all ingredients, cover and chill 24 hours before serving.

*Salsa Verde

10 to 12 tomatillos
2 cups fresh cilantro leaves
2 jalapeno peppers, stemmed, seeded, chopped
½ teaspoon salt

 Peel papery husks off tomatillos. Place in saucepan and add water to cover.

 Bring to boil, lower heat and simmer about 5 minutes. Remove tomatillos and reserve liquid.

 In blender, puree tomatillos with ½ cup reserved liquid, cilantro leaves, jalapeno pepper and salt. Place in bowl with lid and chill.

*Green Chile Salsa

1 (15 ounce) can Mexican-stewed tomatoes
2 (4 ounce) cans chopped green chiles, drained
½ cup chopped green onion with tops
1 clove garlic, minced
2 tablespoons chopped cilantro
1 fresh serrano chile, minced
1 tablespoon lime juice
1 teaspoon oil
½ teaspoon salt

 Drain tomatoes, reserve liquid and chop tomatoes into small pieces.

 In medium bowl, combine tomatoes, remaining ingredients and ¼ cup reserved tomato liquid and chill.

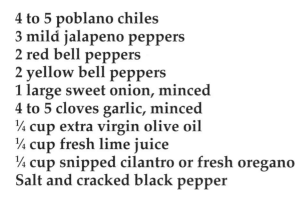

*Roasted Chile Salsa

4 to 5 poblano chiles
3 mild jalapeno peppers
2 red bell peppers
2 yellow bell peppers
1 large sweet onion, minced
4 to 5 cloves garlic, minced
¼ cup extra virgin olive oil
¼ cup fresh lime juice
¼ cup snipped cilantro or fresh oregano
Salt and cracked black pepper

- To roast poblano chiles, hold them over open-flame gas burner or broil them in oven until outside turns dark brown on all sides. (Be careful not to burn holes through skin.)

- Place chiles in plastic bag, seal and allow to sweat for about 15 to 20 minutes so skin will slide off easily. Remove skins and slice through length of chile on one side. Remove seeds, but leave veins intact.

- Follow same roasting procedure for jalapenos and bell peppers. Remove seeds and veins. Chop or mince all peppers.

- Mix all remaining ingredients and serve with fish or chicken.

Roasting green chiles brings out the full flavor of chiles and provides a unique ingredient to Southwest dishes. Green chiles may be used without roasting, but the improvement in flavor is so great, they are roasted the majority of the time.

❊Tomatillo Salsa

1 (13 ounce) can tomatillos
½ cup finely chopped red onion
⅓ cup chopped fresh cilantro
2 or 3 fresh jalapenos, seeded, minced
1 tablespoon lime juice
1 teaspoon olive oil
½ teaspoon salt
¼ teaspoon pepper

❧ Drain tomatillos and combine with all remaining ingredients in food processor.

❧ Process until coarsely chopped and chill overnight before serving.

Tequila Salsa

1 (28 ounce) can diced tomatoes, drained
6 to 8 mild New Mexico green chiles, roasted, peeled, seeded, chopped
½ cup finely chopped onion
⅓ cup chopped fresh cilantro
2 fresh jalapenos, seeded, minced
1 clove garlic, minced
2 tablespoons tequila
1 tablespoon lime juice
1 teaspoon olive oil
½ teaspoon salt

❧ Combine all ingredients in large bowl, mix well and chill several hours or chill overnight before serving.

Sweet Pepper-Jicama Salsa

5 tomatoes, seeded, chopped
1 bunch green onions with tops, chopped
2 jicama, peeled, chopped
1 red bell pepper, seeded, chopped
1 yellow bell pepper, seeded, chopped
1 green bell pepper, seeded, chopped
1 cucumber, peeled, chopped
2 bunches fresh cilantro, snipped
3 cloves garlic, minced
¼ cup canola oil
¼ cup balsamic vinegar
¼ cup lime juice
1 tablespoon cayenne
1 tablespoon cumin
1 teaspoon hot sauce, optional

❦ In large bowl, mix tomatoes, onions, jicama, bell peppers and cucumber and toss gently.

❦ In separate bowl, mix cilantro, garlic, canola oil, vinegar, lime juice, cayenne, cumin and hot sauce and blend well. Pour over vegetables and toss to coat with dressing. Store in closed container in refrigerator and toss occasionally.

As a rule of thumb, the larger the chile, the milder it is. The smaller the chile, the hotter it is. The heat in chiles comes from capsaicin, stored in the oils near the stem, the seeds and veins. The only way to control the degree of heat in chiles is to remove the seeds and veins. Freezing chiles does not affect capsaicin or heat stored in chiles.

*Pico de Gallo

3 whole jalapenos
½ cup minced fresh cilantro
1 bunch green onions with tops, chopped
2 tomatoes, chopped
2 avocados, diced
Juice of 2 limes
½ teaspoon garlic salt
½ teaspoon seasoning salt
¼ teaspoon pepper

 Stem, seed and mince jalapeno. (It is best to use plastic gloves or wash hands immediately after handling jalapenos.)

Add diced jalapenos to large bowl and combine with remaining ingredients.

Chill and serve with tortilla chips or over guacamole salad.

Magic Mango Salsa
This goes great with grilled fish or chicken.

2 ripe mangoes, peeled, chopped
2 tomatoes, seeded, chopped
1 cucumber, seeded, chopped
1 green onion with tops, chopped
1 fresh jalapeno pepper, seeded, veined, chopped
¼ cup snipped fresh cilantro
1 tablespoon lime juice

Mix all ingredients in bowl or container with lid. Chill several hours before serving. Use slotted spoon to serve.

TIP: Make sure you get ripe mangoes and the fruit is sweet next to seed before adding it to the salsa.

*Southwest Ceviche

1 pound flounder, cut in ½-inch pieces
12 to 15 lemons or 1 (15 ounce) bottle lemon or lime juice
4 to 6 large tomatoes, seeded, chopped
2 large green bell pepper, seeded, minced
4 to 6 green onions with tops, minced
5 to 6 green chile peppers, seeded, chopped
½ cup oil
1 cup ketchup
Pinch of oregano

- Marinate flounder in lemon or lime juice for at least 4 hours. (The action of the lemon or lime juice "cooks" fish and turns flounder to opaque color.)

- Add tomatoes, bell peppers, onion, green chiles, oil, ketchup and oregano. (Add green chiles for desired heat.)

- Chill several hours or overnight and serve as appetizer.

Green chiles provide more vitamin C than any other vegetable and twice as much as citrus fruits. As they ripen and turn red, vitamin C decreases and vitamin A increases.

*Stuffed Jalapenos or Green Chiles

1 (11 ounce) can mild jalapenos or 6 to 8 large green chiles
1 (3 ounce) package cream cheese, softened
¼ cup mayonnaise
1 (7 ounce) can white tuna in water, drained
2 tablespoons lemon juice
¼ cup chopped walnuts
Oil

 Slice whole jalapenos in half, remove seeds, drain and soak in ice water.

 In bowl combine cream cheese, mayonnaise, tuna, lemon juice and walnuts and mix well. Shine each jalapeno half with a little oil and stuff each half with cream cheese filling.

TIP: It is a good idea to handle all peppers and chiles with gloves or wash hands thoroughly with soap and water after handling.

*Pickled Jalapenos

1 quart fresh jalapenos   1 cup water
4 cups white vinegar   1 clove garlic
⅓ cup salt   1 jalapeno pepper

 Pack jalapenos in sterilized jars.

 In saucepan, combine vinegar, water, salt, garlic and pepper and bring to boil. Reduce heat and simmer for about 10 minutes.

 Pour over jalapenos and seal jars. Store 2 to 3 weeks before serving.

*Stuffed Jalapenos Con Huevos

1 pound fresh jalapeno peppers
1 (8 ounce) package cream cheese, softened
2 hard-boiled eggs, mashed
½ teaspoon garlic salt
¼ cup finely chopped pecans
1 (2 ounce) can chopped pimentos, drained
Mayonnaise
Paprika

 Halve peppers lengthwise and remove seeds.

 Beat cream cheese with mashed eggs, garlic salt, pecans,
pimentos and seasoning salt. Add enough mayonnaise to
make a paste consistency.

 Fill peppers and mound stuffing slightly. Sprinkle tops
with paprika.

The Southwest region of the United States includes
New Mexico, Arizona, Colorado and the southern
part of Utah. It is a region of diversity and contrasts that
stretches across deserts, mountain ranges, forests, national
wildlife ranges, mesas and vast prairies.

Stuffed Banana Peppers

20 banana peppers
1 (7 ounce) can white meat tuna, well drained, mashed
1 hard-boiled egg, mashed
2 tablespoons minced onion
¼ cup chopped dill pickle
⅓ cup mayonnaise
1 teaspoon prepared mustard
½ teaspoon seasoning salt
½ teaspoon seasoning pepper

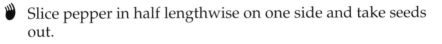

Slice pepper in half lengthwise on one side and take seeds out.

Combine and mix tuna, egg, onion, pickle, mayonnaise, mustard and seasonings.

Fill peppers and chill until ready to serve.

Easy Salsa Dip

1 (8 ounce) jar salsa
1 pint sour cream

Pour salsa into sour cream and mix well. Serve with tortilla chips.

✲Chile Con Queso

2 tablespoons oil
1 tomato, seeded, chopped
1 onion, chopped
2 to 3 serrano chiles, seeded, chopped
2 cloves garlic, minced
½ cup dry white wine
2 (16 ounce) packages shredded cheddar cheese
Tortilla chips

- In large saucepan combine oil, tomato, onion, chiles and garlic. Sprinkle with salt and pepper.

- Saute vegetables over medium heat until onions are soft and translucent (about 5 minutes) and pour into saucepan.

- Add wine and reduce heat to low. Add cheese and stir until it melts. Spoon over tortilla chips and serve immediately.

✲Jalapeno-Bean Dip

1 small onion, minced
1 clove garlic, minced
1 tablespoon oil
1 (15 ounce) can refried beans
1 (12 ounce) package shredded cheddar cheese
1 (4 ounce) can chopped jalapeno peppers, drained

- Saute onion and garlic in oil. Add remaining ingredients and stir over low heat.

- Cook, stirring occasionally, until cheese melts. Transfer to fondue pot or chafing dish to keep warm and serve with chips.

Refried Beans-Avocado Stack

Great fun to eat and a pretty picture too.

1 (15 ounce) can refried beans
½ cup sour cream
⅓ cup mayonnaise
3 avocados
1 lemon
2 tomatoes, diced
4 green onions with tops, chopped
2 (4 ounce) cans diced green chiles
1 clove garlic, minced
1 (10 ounce) jar hot salsa
1 (8 ounce) package shredded Monterey Jack cheese

- Combine refried beans, sour cream and mayonnaise and process in blender. Peel, remove seeds and mash avocados in small bowl. Squeeze lemon over avocados, add juice and mix thoroughly.

- Add tomatoes, green onions, green chiles and garlic to avocados and stir well. Spoon refried bean layer in bottom of 9-inch glass pie plate or make about a 9-inch circle in middle of large platter.

- Spread avocados evenly over top of beans. Pour hot salsa evenly over avocados and top with cheese. Serve with chips or crackers.

Southwest Sizzler Dip

2 (8 ounce) packages cream cheese, softened
¼ cup fresh lime juice
1 tablespoon cumin
1 teaspoon salt
1 teaspoon pepper
1 teaspoon cayenne pepper
1 (8 ounce) can whole kernel corn, drained
1 cup chopped walnuts
1 (4 ounce) can chopped green chiles
3 green onions with tops, chopped

Whip cream cheese until fluffy and beat in lime juice, cumin, salt, pepper and cayenne pepper until smooth.

Stir in corn, walnuts, green chiles and onions and chill overnight. Serve with tortilla chips.

Tipsy Chile Con Queso

2 (16 ounce) packages cubed processed cheese
1 (10 ounce) cans diced green chiles
1 medium onion, chopped
1 (12 ounce) can beer, divided
1 (4 ounce) can taco sauce

In double boiler, melt cheese and stir constantly so cheese will not burn.

Add green chiles, onion, ¼ cup beer and taco sauce and mix well. Thin cheese sauce with a little beer, if needed, and drink the rest. Serve warm with chips.

Layered Taco Dip

½ cup mayonnaise
1 cup sour cream
1 (1½ ounce) package taco seasoning
2 (15 ounce) cans refried beans with green chiles
2 (8 ounce) cartons or pouches prepared guacamole dip
2 tomatoes, chopped
2 green onions with tops, chopped
1 (8 ounce) package shredded cheddar cheese
1 (4 ounce) can chopped ripe olives
Tostados

- Mix mayonnaise, sour cream and taco seasoning and set aside.

- On large platter or 9 x 13-inch baking dish spread refried beans as first layer of dip. Next spread layer of guacamole, layer of sour cream-mayonnaise mixture.

- Sprinkle with chopped tomatoes, green onions, cheese and top with olives. Serve with tostados and chips.

Easy Guacamole Fix

6 to 8 hard, crispy corn tortillas
1 (16 ounce) package prepared guacamole
1 onion, chopped
2 tomatoes, chopped
Salsa

- Place corn tortillas on large platter and spread guacamole on each. Top with onion, tomatoes and salsa and serve.

TIP: See the Salad section on page 88 for more guacamole recipes.

Chicken-Enchilada Dip

2 pounds boneless, skinless chicken thighs, cubed
1 (10 ounce) can enchilada sauce
1 (7 ounce) can chopped green chiles, drained
1 small onion, finely chopped
1 large sweet red bell pepper, finely chopped
2 (8 ounce) packages cream cheese, cubed
1 (16 ounce) package shredded American cheese

- In 4 to 5-quart slow cooker sprayed with vegetable cooking spray, place chicken thighs, enchilada sauce, green chiles, onion and bell pepper.

- Cover and cook on LOW for 4 to 6 hours.

- Stir in cream cheese and American cheese and cook another 30 minutes. Stir several times during cooking. Serve with tortilla chips.

Indian-Corn Dip

1 pound lean ground beef
1 onion, finely chopped
1 (15 ounce) can whole kernel corn, drained
1 (16 ounce) jar salsa
1 (16 ounce) package cubed processed cheese

- In skillet, brown and cook grounded beef on low heat for about 10 minutes and drain. Transfer to slow cooker and add onion, corn, salsa and cheese.

- Cover and cook on LOW for 1 hour; remove lid and stir. Serve with tortilla chips.

*Easy Picadillo

1 pound lean ground beef
1 onion, finely chopped
1 (4 ounce) jar chopped green chiles
1 (2½ ounce) package slivered almonds, toasted
1 teaspoon salt
1 teaspoon black pepper
2 cloves garlic, minced
¾ teaspoon oregano
½ cup water
1 (4 ounce) can chopped ripe olives
1 (4 ounce) can chopped mushrooms
1 (10 ounce) chopped tomatoes and green chiles
1 (1 pound) box processed cheese, cubed

- In large skillet, brown ground beef and drain. Add all remaining ingredients and bring to boil.

- Lower heat and simmer for about 30 minutes. Serve with tortilla chips.

*Chicharrones
It is a lot easier to buy these at the grocery store, but this is the real deal!

2 pounds uncooked pork fat and skins
Salt
Cayenne pepper, optional

- Cut pork fat and skins into 2-inch squares about ¼-inch thick. Put pork squares in cast-iron skillet and cook over medium heat until crispy.

- Remove from skillet and drain on paper towels. Season with salt and cayenne if you want them hot.

Mamacita's Sausage Dip

1 (1 pound) package hot sausage
1 (1 pound) package ground beef
1 onion, chopped
1 (10 ounce) can tomatoes and green chiles
2 (16 ounce) packages cubed processed cheese
1 (10 ounce) can cream of mushroom soup

Brown sausage, ground beef and onion and drain grease.

Add tomatoes and green chiles and mix. Add cheese, cook on low heat and stir until cheese melts.

Add soup concentrate and mix well. Serve hot.

Wild Hog Dip

1 pound hot sausage
1 (10 ounce) can tomatoes and green chiles
1 (1 pound) box processed cheese

Brown sausage and drain fat. Add tomatoes and green chiles, cut cheese into sausage mixture and stir until cheese melts.

Serve in chafing dish with large corn chips.

Tip: This is also great over baked potatoes.

*Tapatias

Tapatias are fried tortillas with any kind of toppings you want. Here are just a few suggestions. Serve them as the main dish, as an appetizer or side dish. They are great any time.

Corn tortillas
Canola oil

TOPPINGS: Choose 1 or More
Refried beans   Chopped onions
Guacamole   Chopped green chiles
Shredded lettuce   Chopped tomatoes
Shredded cheese

In large skillet fry tortillas in a little oil until tortillas are crisp. Drain on paper towels. Spread desired toppings on tortillas and serve.

*Classic Nachos

36 corn tortilla chips
10 pickled jalapeno peppers, sliced
1 cup diced tomatoes, drained
1 (12 ounce) package shredded sharp cheddar cheese
1 (8 ounce) package Monterey Jack cheese
8 green onions with tops, chopped
Guacamole
Salsa

Preheat oven to 450°.

On cookie sheet, arrange chips evenly. Sprinkle with jalapenos, tomatoes and cheeses.

Bake about 5 minutes or until cheese melts. Sprinkle with green onions and serve with spoonful of guacamole or salsa.

*Easy Chalupas

12 flat, crispy corn tortillas
1 (15 ounce) can refried beans
1 (12 ounce) package shredded cheddar cheese
1 cup chopped lettuce
2 tomatoes, chopped
1 large onion, chopped
Salsa

 Preheat oven to 300°.

 Separate tortillas, spread refried beans over each tortilla and sprinkle cheese on top. Place on baking sheets on heat just until cheese melts.

 Remove from oven and top with lettuce, tomato, onion and salsa. Serve immediately.

TIP: *If you cannot find the crispy, flat tortillas, buy the soft ones and heat oil and fry until they are crispy. Drain thoroughly and serve immediately.*

Chapulas are sometimes called Tostadas and are simply open-face sandwiches or snacks on crispy tortillas. Any kind of toppings and dressings will make delicious snacks or meals all-in-one.

APPETIZERS

Shrimp Chalupas

12 flat, crispy corn tortillas
1 cup chopped lettuce
24 large shrimp, cooked, peeled, veined, chopped
1 (15 ounce) can black beans, drained
2 tomatoes, chopped, drained
1 large onion, chopped
Salsa

🖐 Separate tortillas, spread lettuce and shrimp over each tortilla. Add black beans, tomatoes and onions on top.

🖐 Serve with Roasted Chile Salsa on page 22.

*Easy Quesadillas

12 flour tortillas
1 (16 ounce) package shredded cheddar cheese
8 to 10 green chiles, roasted, chopped
Salt
Oil
1 avocado, sliced
Salsa

🖐 Soften tortillas in hot oil and drain. Cover 1 tortilla with cheeses and chiles and sprinkle with salt. Place second tortilla on top. Continue procedure until 6 individual quesadillas are made.

🖐 Place on cookie sheet at 350° and bake until cheese melts. Cut into 4 sections and serve with guacamole and salsa.

Brie Quesadillas

10 flour tortillas
1 pound Brie cheese, cut into ¼-inch strips
½ onion, chopped
2 poblano chiles, roasted, peeled, diced
4 tablespoons butter, melted, mixed with oil
4 tablespoons oil

 Preheat oven to 200°.

 Heat nonstick skillet several minutes and put flour tortillas in for about 15 seconds to soften.

 Put a few strips of cheese, some onions and chiles on half of each tortilla.

 Fold tortillas over and brush on both sides with butter and oil mixture.

 Heat skillet and brown quesadillas on both sides. Place on cookie sheet and store in oven to keep warm while browning remaining quesadillas. Cut each quesadilla into thirds.

Capsaicin, the heat-producing element in chiles, is impervious to cooking times, freezing, drying and storage. The only way to reduce the heat in chiles is to remove the veins and seeds. Be sure to use rubber gloves when handling chiles.

Easy Poblano-Corn Tortilla Quesadillas

6 to 8 poblano chile peppers
24 corn tortillas
4 to 6 (16 ounce) packages shredded Mexican-cheese blend
4 large tomatoes, seeded, chopped
2 large onions, chopped
Salsa

🖐 Roast poblano chile peppers over open-flame gas burner or broil them in oven until outside turns dark brown on all sides. (Be careful not to burn holes through skin.)

🖐 Place peppers in plastic bag and seal for about 15 to 20 minutes to sweat so skins will slide off easily. Remove skins and slice through length of pepper on one side. Remove seeds, but leave veins intact.

🖐 Slice pepper into long strips and place several on half of tortilla.

🖐 Add cheese to within ½ inch of edges, fold over and cook on griddle at 350° until cheese melts.

🖐 Repeat process with all remaining tortillas.

🖐 Turn to other side with spatula and cook just until cheese begins to seep out edges. Serve immediately with tomatoes, onions and salsa.

TIP: If tortillas break easily, wrap about 5 of them in slightly damp paper towel and microwave for about 45 seconds. This will soften them enough to fold without breaking.

Quesadillas With Goat Cheese And Nopalitos

Nopalitos, the small pads of prickly pear cactus, add a wonderful complimentary flavor to the goat cheese.

6 New Mexico green chiles, roasted, peeled, seeded
6 flour tortillas
1 (16 ounce) carton goat cheese
1 (15 ounce) jar nopalitos
2 avocados, sliced

 Cut chiles into strips. Lay 2 tortillas in large skillet and sprinkle goat cheese to within ½ inch of edges. Add nopalitos, avocados and chiles over cheese and top with flour tortilla.

Heat until cheese begins to melt or tortilla browns slightly. Turn to other side and heat until cheese melts. Cut into wedges and serve immediately.

Tortilla De Queso

2 (8 ounce) packages cream cheese, softened
1 (4 ounce) can chopped green chiles
1 bunch green onions with tops, chopped
1 clove garlic, finely minced
½ teaspoon salt
12 flour tortillas

Combine and mix cream cheese, green chiles, green onions, garlic and salt.

Spread layer of cream cheese mixture on each tortilla. Roll and slice tortillas into bite-size pieces.

✿Porker Taquitos
These "little tacos" are great with chicken or beef.

2 pounds lean ground pork sausage
½ teaspoon seasoning salt
¼ teaspoon pepper
½ teaspoon oregano
1 clove garlic, minced
2 medium onions, chopped
2 (16 ounce) packages shredded, sharp cheddar cheese
1 teaspoon salt
1 teaspoon ground cumin
24 fresh green chiles, roasted, seeded, peeled
24 egg-roll wrappers

 In skillet brown pork sausage and drain excess grease. Add seasoning salt, pepper, oregano, garlic and onions and cook until onions are translucent.

 Remove from heat, add cheese, salt and cumin and stir well.

🖐 Dry each chile and cut open. Spoon about 2 tablespoons meat mixture inside chile and close.

🖐 Lay out each egg-roll wrapper and place filled chile diagonally across wrapper. Wrap each chile with wrapper by tucking lower triangle flap over and under chile. Bring left and right corners toward the center to seal and roll. Seal edges with a little water.

🖐 Deep fry at 325° until golden brown. Drain on paper towels and serve immediately.

TIP: Substitute 2 pounds boneless, skinless, chicken breast halves, cooked and shredded instead of pork. For another flavor, try 2 pounds lean ground beef, browned and drained instead of chicken or pork.

✡Chicken Flautas

Flautas are rolled tacos. Corn tortillas, sometimes flour tortillas, are filled with meat mixture, rolled tightly and fried.

4 to 6 boneless, skinless chicken breast halves, cooked, shredded
1 clove garlic, minced
2 medium onions, chopped
1 to 2 fresh green chiles, roasted, peeled, seeded, chopped
Oil
12 corn tortillas

❥ Mix chicken, garlic, onions and chiles well. Heat tortillas in non-stick skillet to soften. Place filling down center of tortilla and roll tightly. Secure with toothpick and fry in hot oil in skillet. Drain and serve.

Plantain-Sweet Potato Chips

3 medium sweet potatoes
3 medium plantains, peeled, cut into ¼-inch slices
Vegetable oil
Chile powder
Salt

❥ Peel potatoes, slice into ¹⁄₁₆-inch slices and put in bowl with ice water. Heat about 2 to 3 inches oil in heavy skillet or Dutch oven. Carefully place plantains in oil and fry until golden brown. Drain on paper towel and sprinkle with chile powder and salt.

❥ Drain potatoes and dry with paper towel. Carefully place plantains in oil and fry until golden brown. Drain on paper towel and sprinkle with salt. Serve at room temperature.

*Chiles Rellenos

½ cup shredded sharp cheddar cheese
½ cup shredded Monterey Jack cheese
10 large green chiles, roasted, peeled, seeded
½ cup flour
1 teaspoon salt
2 eggs, beaten
Oil

 Mix both cheeses in small bowl and set aside.

 Lay chiles flat, slice through flesh of chile on one side and stuff with cheeses. Close chile, roll in flour and salt and dip in beaten eggs.

 Place each chile relleno in large skillet with a little, very hot oil and splash hot oil over top to form a crust. When side is brown, turn with spatula. Drain on paper towel and serve warm.

TIP: Roll chiles in flour and dust off excess. Flour makes the seam stay together so stuffing does not leak.

TIP: Roasting Chiles-page 9.

Remedies for Hot Peppers:
If you eat a pepper that is too hot for comfort, try drinking a glass of milk. A glass of ice water only disperses the oil from the capsaicin in the mouth and does little to tame the heat.

Albuquerque Chile Rellenos

4 to 6 fresh whole green chiles
1 (16 ounce) block Monterey Jack cheese
1 (16 ounce) package shredded cheddar cheese
Paprika
5 large eggs, beaten
¼ cup flour
1¼ cups milk
½ teaspoon salt
½ teaspoon pepper
1 teaspoon cayenne pepper

 Preheat oven to 350°.

 Cut each chile on 1 side lengthwise, remove seeds and set aside.

 Cut block cheese in 14 to 16 slices and put 1 slice in each chile. Put chiles side by side in prepared 9 x 13-inch baking dish or smaller dish if needed. Sprinkle grated cheese and paprika over chiles and set aside.

 In medium bowl, beat eggs and flour until smooth consistency. Add milk, salt, pepper, cayenne pepper and mix thoroughly.

 Pour egg mixture over chiles and bake uncovered 45 minutes or until dish is firm in middle.

Chile Relleno Bites

2 pounds pork tenderloin or lean pork
3 cloves garlic, minced
1 to 2 cups fresh green chiles, roasted, diced
1 (16 ounce) package cubed processed cheese
6 hard-boiled eggs, minced
¾ cup flour
Canola oil
2 eggs, beaten

❦ Use food processor to chop pork into very small pieces,
   put into large skillet and brown. Add garlic and chiles to
   mixture and cook for about 5 to 10 minutes over low heat.

❦ Remove from heat and add cheese to skillet. Stir until
   cheese melts and add hard-boiled eggs. Mix gently.

❦ Chill several hours or overnight. Remove from
   refrigerator, shape into small balls or logs, coat with flour
   and return to refrigerator.

❦ In deep fryer or skillet, heat oil, coat each piece in beaten
   egg and fry. Turn pieces gently. When golden color,
   remove from heat, drain and serve warm.

The heat from chile peppers is found in the capsaicin
under the stem and in the seeds and veins. If you want
to reduce the heat in chiles, remove the seeds and veins.

New Mexico Cheese Squares

10 eggs
½ cup flour
1 teaspoon baking powder
½ teaspoon salt
½ cup (1 stick) butter, melted
1 (7 ounce) can chopped, pickled jalapeno peppers
1 (16 ounce) carton small curd cottage cheese
1 (16 ounce) package shredded Monterey Jack cheese

🐝 Preheat oven to 350° and grease 9 x 13-inch baking pan.

🐝 In mixing bowl, beat eggs, add flour, baking powder and salt and mix well. Add butter, peppers, cottage cheese and Monterey Jack cheese. Mix and pour into baking pan.

🐝 Bake uncovered for about 50 minutes. Test with knife in center of quiche for doneness. Knife should come out clean. Cut in bite-size squares and serve hot or warm.

Jalapeno-Cheese Squares

1 (4 ounce) can chopped jalapeno peppers, drained
1 (16 ounce) package shredded cheddar cheese
6 eggs, beaten

🐝 Preheat oven to 350°. Grease or spray 9 x 9-inch baking pan.

🐝 Spread jalapenos on bottom and sprinkle cheese evenly over peppers.

🐝 Pour eggs in baking dish and bake uncovered for 30 minutes or until firm. Serve hot.

Taco Pie

1 (15 ounce) can refried beans
3 ripe avocados
3 tablespoons lemon juice
¼ cup hot salsa
1 (16 ounce) carton sour cream
1 (1 ounce) package dry taco seasoning mix
1 (8 ounce) package shredded Monterey Jack cheese
1 (8 ounce) package shredded Colby cheese
3 tomatoes, peeled, seeded, chopped, drained
1 bunch green onions with top, chopped

💓 Spread beans inside prepared 10-inch springform pan.

💓 Peel, seed and mash avocados with fork and mix with lemon juice and salsa. Spread over refried beans.

💓 Combine and mix sour cream and taco seasoning mix and spread over avocados.

💓 Sprinkle both cheeses over sour cream layer and top with tomatoes and green onions. Chill about 5 hours before serving.

💓 Remove sides from pan and place bottom of springform pan on serving platter. Serve with chips.

Hatch, New Mexico is located in the south central part of the state and is considered the most famous area for chile production. In September all the stores in Hatch sell fresh-roasted green chiles and the rest of the year they sell chiles that are dried, canned or ground into powder.

49

Tortilla Pinwheels

1 (8 ounce) package cream cheese, softened
1 (4 ounce) can chopped green chiles, drained
1 (4 ounce) can chopped ripe olives, drained
5 to 6 dashes hot sauce
½ teaspoon garlic powder
10 flour tortillas
10 thin slices cooked chicken

- Stir cream cheese, add green chiles, ripe olives, hot sauce and garlic and mix well.

- Spread mixture on flour tortillas. Place chicken slice on tortilla and roll up tightly. Wrap in plastic wrap and chill for 2 to 3 hours.

- To serve remove plastic wrap and slice into 1-inch pieces.

Chile-Cheese Ball

1 (16 ounce) package grated sharp cheddar cheese
1 (8 ounce) package cream cheese, softened
1 tablespoon worcestershire sauce
1 tablespoon mayonnaise
½ teaspoon salt
¼ teaspoon garlic powder
½ cup finely chopped pecans
Chile powder

- In mixing bowl, beat cheddar cheese, cream cheese, worcestershire, mayonnaise, salt and garlic powder.

- Roll mixture into large ball and sprinkle thoroughly with chile powder. Roll in pecans and serve with crackers or chips.

*Homemade Tostados

Chips are easy to buy, but these really taste great.

12 corn tortillas
Canola oil
Salt

 With kitchen shears or sharp knife, cut tortillas in pie-shape pieces to the size you want. In cast-iron skillet or heavy skillet, heat oil and put in tortilla pieces.

 Cook until tortillas are crisp, remove from skillet and drain on paper towels. Sprinkle salt over chips while they are still hot.

*Green Chile Jelly

1 cup diced fresh green chiles or 3 (4 ounce) cans diced green chiles
2 cups sugar
¼ cup cider vinegar
½ cup water
1 (2 ounce) package fruit pectin

 In small saucepan combine green chiles, sugar, vinegar, water and fruit pectin and bring to boil.

 Stir well to dissolve sugar. Remove from heat and cool.

 Pour into glass jars and serve over cream cheese with crackers.

51

Fruit Punch Olé

1 quart fresh orange juice
1 (6 ounce) can frozen pineapple juice concentrate, thawed
½ cup lemon juice
1 cup tequila
½ cup triple sec
1 quart club soda, chilled
1 pint orange sherbert

- Combine orange juice, pineapple juice concentrate, water, lemon juice, tequila and triple sec in very large bowl or 1-gallon jar, mix well and refrigerate.

- When ready to serve, pour mixture in punch bowl. Stir in club soda and place scoops of sherbet in punch to float.

*Mexican Hot Chocolate

¼ cup cocoa
¼ cup sugar
½ teaspoon cinnamon
¼ teaspoon nutmeg
⅓ cup water
3½ cups milk
1 teaspoon vanilla
4 cinnamon sticks

- Combine cocoa, sugar, cinnamon, nutmeg and water in saucepan. Cook, stirring occasionally, over medium heat until cocoa powder and sugar dissolve.

- Add milk and vanilla, heat to simmering and whip mixture with hand beater until frothy. Pour into mugs and place cinnamon stick in each mug.

*Spanish Coffee

¾ cup kahlua
2 tablespoons sugar
4 cups hot brewed coffee
Whipped cream
Chocolate curls

Stir kahlua and sugar into hot coffee. Pour into 4 coffee mugs and top each serving with dollop of whipped cream. Garnish with chocolate curls.

*Sangrita
This is the Mexican version of a Bloody Mary.

6 ounces tomato juice
5 to 6 drops onion juice
5 to 6 drops jalapeno juice
Worcestershire sauce
2 ounces tequila

Mix all ingredients well. Pour over ice and serve.

The staples of the Indians who roamed Mexico and the New World were chile peppers, beans, corn and squash. From these basic ingredients, regional cuisines in Mexico and America developed into an art form.

*Sangria

1 quart (4 cups) red table wine
1 quart (1 liter) club soda
1 cup water
2 oranges, divided
2 lemons
2 limes
1 cup sugar
Crush Ice

 In large pitcher pour red wine, club soda, water, juice of 1 orange, juice of lemons and limes and stir well. Cut remaining orange into ¼-slices and put several slices into pitcher.

 Add sugar and crushed ice and stir well. Pour into glasses and put 1 slice orange on rim of each glass before serving.

Southwest Pina Colada

1 (8 ounce) can crushed pineapple with liquid
1 (7 ounce) can cream of coconut
1 cup rum
Ice cubes

 Combine all ingredients in blender, except ice and mix. Add enough ice for desired consistency and process until liquid is "slushy". Serve while ice cold.

*Simple Margarita

2 limes, divided
Coarse salt
1 cup tequila
1 cup triple sec
1 cup fresh lime juice
Crushed ice

- Squeeze juice from 1 lime into saucer, dip rim of glasses into juice from 1 lime just to dampen. Dip rim into coarse salt and dry.

- In glass pitcher combine tequila, triple sec and lime juice and stir well. Pour into rim-salted glasses and serve. Garnish with slices of lime.

Margaritas

Lime juice for glasses
Coarse salt
½ cup tequila
2 tablespoons triple sec
¼ cup lime juice
2 tablespoons powdered sugar
2 cups crushed ice

- To prepare salt rim on glasses, dip rim of glass into ¼ inch lime juice, then into shallow dish of coarse salt. Shake off excess salt and dry at room temperature.

- To make margarita, combine tequila, triple sec, lime juice, powdered sugar and crushed ice. Blend until very frothy. Serve in glasses with rims dipped in coarse salt.

Margarita Freeze
Great for the freezer and instant margaritas!

1 (16 ounce) container sweet and sour liquid bar mix or
3 (6 ounce) cans limeade
12 ounces tequila
6 ounces triple sec

- In large plastic container with lid mix all ingredients and freeze. Liquid will be slushy. Dip or pour into margarita glasses.

Quick Kahlua

8 cups water
10 tablespoons coffee
2½ cups sugar
4 tablespoons Mexican vanilla
1½ cups bourbon

- Make a pot of coffee using 8 cups water and 10 tablespoons coffee. Pour coffee into large saucepan, add sugar and bring to boil. Lower heat and simmer about 45 minutes.

- Add vanilla, cool to room temperature then add bourbon. This may be stored in jars at room temperature. Serve in cordial glasses or over ice cream.

BRUNCHES
& BREADS

*Burritos

Burritos are flour tortillas filled with any of several ingredients. They may be served any time of day with any kind of filling. Here are just a few suggestions.

Flour tortillas
Fillings:

Refried beans	**Shredded meats**
Chile con carne	**Potatoes**
Chile con queso	**Onions**
Scrambled eggs	**Chiles**
Guacamole	**Salsa**

Wrap flour tortilla in dry paper towel and cook it in microwave for about 10 seconds. Choose fillings and put in middle of flour tortilla. Fold 4 sides toward center like an envelope and eat with hands or fork.

*Sausage and Egg Burritos

1 pound bulk pork sausage
10 eggs, well beaten
3 tablespoons milk
1 (8 ounce) package shredded Mexican 4-cheese blend
10 to 12 flour tortillas

Brown sausage in large skillet and cook until meat turns brown. Drain and move sausage to one side of skillet. Combine eggs and milk and pour into other side of skillet.

Scramble eggs and stir constantly to keep eggs from sticking and burning. When eggs are almost firm, mix with sausage.

Remove from heat and scoop eggs-sausage mixture into each flour tortilla. Add 1 tablespoon salsa and roll up tortilla. Serve immediately.

58

*Egg-Cheese Burritos

¼ cup (½ stick) butter
6 eggs, well beaten
3 tablespoons milk
2 New Mexico green chiles, roasted, peeled, chopped
4 green onions with tops, chopped
1 (8 ounce) package shredded Mexican 4-cheese blend
Flour tortillas
Salsa

- In large omelet pan or skillet, melt butter, beat eggs with milk and pour into skillet. Scramble eggs in skillet and stir constantly to keep eggs from sticking and burning.

- When eggs are almost firm, sprinkle onions, chiles and cheese over eggs and stir. Remove from heat and scoop eggs into flour tortilla. Add salsa and roll up tortilla. Serve immediately.

Easy Huevos

1 (14 ounce) can taco sauce
8 eggs
6 flour tortillas

- In small saucepan, simmer taco sauce. In large skillet sprayed with cooking spray, fry or scramble eggs and put on flour tortilla.

- Spoon about 2 tablespoons taco sauce on each tortilla, roll up and serve hot.

*Southwestern Huevos Rancheros

The traditional version of Huevos Rancheros in the Southwest uses poached eggs and the basic Red Chile Sauce used on so many Southwestern dishes.

8 to 10 New Mexico dried red chiles
2 cups water
1 onion, chopped
1 teaspoon minced garlic
1 tomato, finely chopped, drained
6 corn tortillas
6 eggs

 Preheat oven to 350°.

 Place dried chiles on baking pan and cook in oven at 250° until chiles blister, but do not burn. Remove stems and seeds. Crush or crumble chiles in saucepan with water and add onion, garlic and tomato.

 Bring to boil, reduce heat and simmer for about 30 minutes or until desired thickness. Pour into blender and puree mixture.

 Fry each tortilla in a little hot oil until soft. Pour sauce in large skillet with lid on low heat. Crack eggs in the sauce and cover with lid. Poach eggs until yolks are partially done.

 To serve, place tortilla on serving plate or individual plates, spoon about ⅓ cup sauce over each tortilla and gently slip eggs onto tortilla. Serve hot.

*Huevos Rancheros

This is another version of Huevos Rancheros using fried eggs instead of poached eggs.

½ cup chopped onion
½ teaspoon minced garlic
3 tablespoons bacon drippings
4 tomatoes, seeded, finely chopped, drained
Minced jalapenos peppers to taste
½ teaspoon salt
6 eggs
6 fried tortillas

Saute onion and garlic in bacon drippings. Add tomatoes, peppers and salt. Cover and simmer until sauce thickens.

Fry each egg over-easy or sunny-side up and place one on each tortilla. Spoon sauce over each egg and serve.

Indian communities are active today along the Rio Grande in Santa Clara, Taos, Cochiti, Santo Domingo, Isleta and Tesuque. These Pueblo people are descendants of the Anasazi people, the Ancient Ones, who built thousands of massive, castle-like villages throughout the Southwest. While most speak English, they maintain their individual Indian cultures and languages. As examples, the Acoma people practice secret rites dating back to their ancestors who inhabited the Mesa Verde compounds and are closed to everyone except their tribe. The Zuni people follow an ancient kachina religion. Both tribes speak in their native languages.

Conquistador Green Chile Quiche

4 to 5 slices bacon, fried crisp
1 (9-inch) unbaked piecrust
4 eggs, beaten well
2 cups half-and-half cream
2 tablespoons chopped onion
1 (4 ounce) can diced green chiles
1 (8 ounce) package shredded Swiss cheese

- Preheat oven to 350°. Crumble bacon and spread half in piecrust. In large bowl combine beaten eggs, cream, onion, green chiles, cheese and salt and pour evenly into piecrusts.

- Sprinkle remaining bacon on top. Bake for 40 to 45 minutes or until light brown on top.

Sunrise Cheese Squares

10 eggs
½ cup flour
1 teaspoon baking powder
½ cup (1 stick) butter, melted
1 (7 ounce) can chopped jalapeno peppers
1 (16 ounce) carton small curd cottage cheese
1 (16 ounce) package grated Monterey Jack cheese

- Preheat oven to 350° and grease 9 x 13-inch baking pan. In mixing bowl, beat eggs, add flour, baking powder and salt and mix well. Add butter, peppers, cottage cheese and Monterey Jack cheese. Mix well and pour into baking pan.

- Bake uncovered for about 50 minutes. Test with knife in center of squares for doneness. Knife should come out clean. Cut in bite-size squares and serve hot or warm.

Sonora Desert Omelet

¼ cup (½ stick) butter
6 eggs, well beaten
3 tablespoons milk
4 green onions with tops, chopped
1 (4 ounce) can diced green chiles, drained
1 tablespoon pickled jalapeno slices, drained
1 (8 ounce) package shredded Mexican 4-cheese blend
Salt and pepper
Salsa
Flour tortillas

In large omelet pan or skillet melt butter and pour in well beaten eggs and milk. Swirl eggs in pan so eggs cook from the bottom.

When eggs are almost firm, sprinkle onions, chiles, jalapenos and cheese on half of eggs. As cheese begins to melt, flip other side of eggs on top of onion mixture.

Serve when cheese melts and eggs are fully cooked. Serve hot with salsa and heated flour tortillas.

The pueblos of the Acoma and Zuni people are in the northwestern part of New Mexico. These people have been living in this area since before Columbus discovered to the New World.

Cheesy Jalapeno Quiche

1 (9 inch) unbaked piecrust
1 cup chopped, cooked ham
1 (8 ounce) package shredded colby cheese
1 (8 ounce) package shredded cheddar cheese
¼ onion, chopped
2 pickled or fresh jalapeno peppers, seeded, chopped
¼ cup minced fresh parsley
6 eggs, beaten
1 teaspoon dry mustard
½ cup sour cream

🖐 Preheat oven to 350°.

🖐 In unbaked piecrust layer ham, both cheeses, onion, jalapenos and parsley.

🖐 In bowl combine eggs, mustard and sour cream and mix well. Pour over ham and cheeses. Bake for 35 minutes or until filling is firm in center. Let quiche stand for about 5 minutes before serving.

The Apache and Navajo nations are descendants of the nomadic Athabascans who traveled from the far north along the Rocky Mountains to the south. Today, the Navajo nation is the largest Indian tribe in the U.S.

Green Chile-Sausage Quiche

1 (7 ounce) can whole green chiles, drained
1 (9 inch) unbaked piecrust
1 pound hot sausage, cooked, crumbled
4 eggs, crumbled
1 pint half-and-half cream
½ cup grated parmesan cheese
¾ cup grated Monterey Jack cheese
½ teaspoon salt
¼ teaspoon pepper

 Preheat oven to 350°.

 Split and seed green chiles and place in piecrust. Sprinkle cooked, crumbled sausage over chiles. In bowl combine eggs, cream, both cheeses, salt and pepper and pour over sausage.

 Bake for 35 minutes or until top is golden brown. Let stand for 5 minutes before serving.

The Navajo Nation is the largest and fastest growing Indian tribe in the U.S. with more than 200,000 people scattered across its reservation. Many of the Navajo people choose to live in the traditional ways and build their homes far from main roads and other houses. The Nation controls most of the northwest quadrant of New Mexico. The reservation is larger than Massachusetts, Connecticut and Vermont combined.

Four Corners Breakfast Casserole

2 (4 ounce) cans diced green chiles
1 (16 ounce) package shredded Monterey Jack cheese
1 (16 ounce) package shredded cheddar cheese
4 eggs, separated
1 (5 ounce) can evaporated milk
1 tablespoon flour
½ teaspoon salt
3 tomatoes, sliced

 Preheat oven to 350°.

 In prepared 9 x 13-inch casserole dish, combine green chiles, Monterey Jack cheese and cheddar cheese.

 In large bowl, blend egg yolks, milk, flour and salt. In separate bowl, beat egg whites until stiff and fold into egg yolk mixture. Pour egg mixture over cheeses and stir slightly with fork.

 Bake for 30 minutes, remove from oven and cover top with sliced tomatoes. Return to oven and bake an additional 20 to 30 minutes.

Green chiles are considered vegetables in the Southwest and no other vegetable has had a greater effect on a way of life and a way of cooking than the chiles of the Southwest. Chiles are used fresh, canned, dried, roasted, minced, pureed and stuffed whole.

Route 66 Chile-Cheese Pie

1 (9 inch) piecrust, baked
1½ cups crumbled guacamole-flavored tortilla chips, divided
1 (15 ounce) can chili beans
2 (4 ounce) cans diced green chiles, drained
3 green onions with tops, chopped
1 (4 ounce) can sliced black olives, drained
½ cup sour cream
1 (4 ounce) can sliced mushrooms, drained
1 (8 ounce) package shredded Mexican 4-cheese blend

🌶 Preheat oven to 350°.

🌶 In piecrust, line bottom with 1 cup crumbled chips. In
bowl combine beans, green chiles, onions and olives and
spread evenly over chips.

🌶 Put layer of sour cream next and sprinkle mushrooms
on top. Sprinkle evenly with cheese and final layer of
remaining chips.

🌶 Cover dish with foil and bake for about 15 minutes.
Uncover and bake another 15 to 20 minutes longer until
well heated. Serve immediately.

Route 66, also known as "America's Main Street", runs
through New Mexico and Arizona. The longest stretch
of the original Route 66 remaining is found in Arizona.
The road was officially opened in 1926 and was the road
depicted in John Steinbeck's "Grapes of Wrath" showing
Oklahoma farmers traveling west to California during the
drought of the 1930's.

Canyon Strata

6 slices white bread
Butter
1 (12 ounce) package shredded cheddar cheese
1 (12 ounce) package shredded Monterey Jack cheese
1 (7 ounce) can chopped green chiles, drained
6 eggs
2 cups half-and-half cream
1 teaspoon salt
½ teaspoon paprika
1 teaspoon flaked oregano
¼ teaspoon black pepper
½ teaspoon garlic powder
¼ teaspoon dry mustard

 Preheat oven to 325°.

🖐 Trim crusts from bread and spread one side with butter. Arrange bread, butter side down, in 9 x 13-inch baking dish. Sprinkle cheeses over bread and distribute chiles evenly over cheese layer.

🖐 In bowl beat eggs with half-and-half, salt, paprika, oregano, pepper, garlic powder and dry mustard and pour over casserole.

🖐 Cover with foil and chill overnight or at least 5 hours. Bake uncovered for 50 minutes or until top browns lightly. Let stand 10 minutes before serving.

*Anytime Enchiladas

1 (12 ounce) carton small curd cottage cheese, drained
1½ cups sour cream, divided
½ teaspoon salt
½ teaspoon pepper
1 (14 ounce) can enchilada sauce
1 (8 ounce) block cheddar cheese
12 tortillas
1 (14 ounce) can diced green chiles
1 (8 ounce) package shredded Mexican 4-cheese blend
1 (4 ounce) can chopped black olives, drained

- Preheat oven to 350°.

- Combine cottage cheese, ½ cup sour cream, salt and pepper in small bowl and set aside. Combine enchilada sauce and ½ cup sour cream in separate bowl and set aside.

- Cut block of cheese into 12 slices and set aside. Prepare 9 x 13-inch baking dish with cooking spray.

- Lay several tortillas flat and spoon about 1 tablespoon cottage cheese-sour cream mixture in middle of each tortilla.

- Add 1 slice cheese and about 1 tablespoon green chiles. Roll up tortilla and place, seam-side down, in baking dish. Repeat process with all tortillas.

- Pour enchilada sauce mixture over all tortillas in baking dish. Sprinkle cheese, olives and remaining sour cream over top. Bake for 25 to 30 minutes or until enchiladas are heated thoroughly.

✷Chile-Cheese Grits

6 cups water
1½ cups uncooked grits
1 (16 ounce) package shredded cheddar cheese
¼ cup (½ stick) butter
3 eggs, well beaten
1 teaspoon seasoned salt
1 teaspoon salt
½ teaspoon hot sauce
1 (4 ounce) can chopped green chiles
Paprika

 Preheat oven to 275°.

Bring water to boil, add grits slowly and cook until done. Add cheese and butter and stir until both melt. Fold in beaten eggs, seasoned salt, salt, hot sauce and green chiles.

Pour into greased 9 x 13-inch baking pan. Bake for 1 hour 20 minutes. (If center is not set, cook a little longer.) When serving, sprinkle a little paprika on top.

Tip: This may be prepared ahead of time and baked right before serving.

Grits are ground white hominy pieces that may be eaten as a cereal or cooked with chiles and cheese as a side dish.

*Southwest-Jalapeno Cornbread

2½ cups yellow cornmeal
1 cup flour
2 tablespoons sugar
1 tablespoon salt
4 teaspoons baking powder
3 eggs, room temperature
½ cup oil
1½ cups buttermilk
1 (15 ounce) can cream-style corn
6 to 8 jalapeno peppers, seeded, chopped
¼ cup chopped bell pepper
1 (16 ounce) package grated cheddar cheese
1 onion, finely chopped
3 slices bacon, cooked, crumbled

 Preheat oven to 375°.

 Combine cornmeal, flour, sugar, salt and baking powder
   and stir well. Add eggs, oil and buttermilk and mix well.

 Stir in creamed corn, jalapenos, bell peppers, cheese, onion
   and bacon and mix well. Pour into 9 x 13-inch baking dish
   and bake for 45 minutes or until lightly browned.

Ancestral Puebloan people began building elaborate
dwellings that became villages. Around 800 A.D. the
Chaca Canyon area in the Four Corners was the site of one
of the most impressive Pre-Columbian villages in North
America. Mesa Verde, built around 1000 A.D., is the site of
some of the best preserved and most elaborate of the cliff
dwellings built by Puebloan people.

Green Chile-Corn Fritters

3 teaspoons baking powder
1½ cups flour
1 teaspoon sugar
½ teaspoon salt
1 egg, beaten
1 (4 ounce) can chopped green chiles, drained
1 (8 ounce) can whole kernel corn, drained
Milk
Oil for frying

🌶 Sift dry ingredients in bowl. Add egg, green chiles, corn and enough milk to make batter consistency.

🌶 Mix well and drop batter from tablespoon into hot oil and fry until golden brown. Makes about 2 dozen.

Cast-Iron Chile Pepper Cornbread

3 cups cornbread mix
3 eggs, beaten
2½ cups milk
1 large onion, grated
½ cup chopped jalapeno chiles, seeded
1 (12 ounce) package shredded cheddar cheese
6 slices bacon, cooked, crumbled
½ cup bacon drippings
½ cup chopped pimento, drained
1 cup cream-style corn
1 clove garlic, minced

🌶 Preheat oven to 375°.

🌶 Mix all ingredients and pour into 2 large cast-iron skillets. Bake for about 35 to 40 minutes or until cornbread tests done in center.

Skillet Cornbread

1 cup flour
1 cup yellow or blue cornmeal
1 tablespoon baking powder
1 teaspoon salt
¼ cup sugar
2 eggs
1 cup milk
¼ cup oil
Oil for frying

🖐 Combine flour, cornmeal, baking powder, salt and sugar in large bowl. Stir in eggs, milk and ¼ cup oil.

🖐 Heat oil for frying in cast-iron or heavy skillet. Shape cornbread into small patties about ½ to 1 inch thick and fry in oil.

🖐 Turn once and brown on both sides. Remove from skillet, drain on paper towel and serve hot.

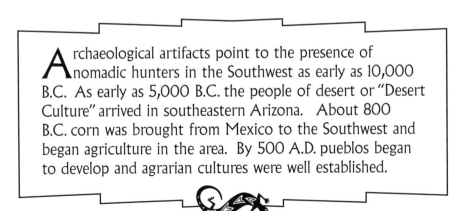

Archaeological artifacts point to the presence of nomadic hunters in the Southwest as early as 10,000 B.C. As early as 5,000 B.C. the people of desert or "Desert Culture" arrived in southeastern Arizona. About 800 B.C. corn was brought from Mexico to the Southwest and began agriculture in the area. By 500 A.D. pueblos began to develop and agrarian cultures were well established.

Corn Sticks

These are just great with soup!

1½ cups flour
1 cup yellow cornmeal
1 teaspoon baking powder
¼ teaspoon salt
½ cup (1 stick) butter, softened
1 (8 ounce) package shredded cheddar cheese
2 eggs
⅓ cup milk

Preheat oven to 375°.

Mix flour, cornmeal, baking powder and salt in bowl. Cut in butter with pastry blender, stir well to make mixture resemble coarse crumbs.

Stir in cheese, eggs and milk until soft dough forms. Cover and chill until dough is firm enough to roll out, about 30 minutes.

On lightly floured surface, pat dough with hands and roll out with rolling pin about ⅓ inch thick. Cut in ½-inch strips and trim each strip to about 3 inches long.

Place 1 inch apart on greased cookie sheet. Bake for about 30 minutes or until lightly browned. Serve hot with butter.

The Navajo and Apache peoples descended from the Athabascans from Canada and Alaska who traveled south along the Rocky Mountains. The Navajo came to the Southwest sometime around 1200 A.D. and the Apaches came to the area in the late 15th century.

Vegetable-Cornbread Muffins

1¼ cups yellow cornmeal
¾ cup flour
¼ cup shortening
1½ cups buttermilk
2 teaspoons baking powder
1 tablespoon sugar
1 teaspoon salt
½ teaspoon baking soda
2 eggs
1 cup shredded zucchini, drained
½ cup chopped red bell pepper
2 tablespoons seeded, chopped serrano chiles or jalapenos

🖐 Preheat oven to 400°.

🖐 Greases 16 to 18 muffing cups. (Do not use paper cups because they stick.)

🖐 Mix cornmeal and flour in mixing bowl and cut shortening into cornmeal and flour. Add all other ingredients except zucchini, bell pepper and chiles and beat well for 30 seconds.

🖐 Stir in remaining ingredients. Fill muffin cups almost full and bake about 25 to 30 or until golden brown. Remove from pan immediately.

TIP: Serrano chiles are hotter than jalapenos, so if you would like a milder flavor, try jalapenos.

*Homemade Flour Tortillas

2 tablespoons bacon drippings
2 cups flour
1 teaspoon salt
1 teaspoon baking powder
¼ to ½ cup water

- Heat bacon drippings in cast-iron skillet or heavy skillet to pouring consistency.

- Combine flour, salt and baking powder in medium bowl.

- Pour bacon drippings into flour mixture and stir well. Add water, a little at a time, to reach firm, but pliable consistency. Cover bowl with towel for 5 to 10 minutes.

- Pull out dough about the size of golf ball and press out to flat, round tortilla about 6 to 7 inches in diameter and about ¼ inch thick.

- Heat cast-iron or heavy, non-stick skillet and place each tortilla in skillet. Cook until each side browns slightly and transfer to paper towel.

- Place each tortilla on separate paper towels to keep tortillas from "sweating". Serve hot with butter or cool and serve any time.

Hopi Indian pueblos are said to be the oldest continually occupied towns in North America.

*Homemade Corn Tortillas

3 cups masa harina
1¾ to 2 cups hot water

 Mix masa harina with a little water until you can form it into large, soft ball.

 Cover bowl with cup towel and take out enough dough to make smaller balls about 2 inches in diameter. Keep bowl covered to keep moisture in dough. Add water if necessary.

 Put small ball in between 2 pieces of plastic wrap and roll out flat to about 6 to 7 inches in diameter and about ¼ inch thick. Seal plastic wrap so dough will not dry out.

 Heat heavy skillet or griddle with a little oil and remove plastic from tortilla before putting in hot oil.

 Cook in hot oil for about 30 seconds, then turn to other side and cook for another 30 seconds or until tortillas appear to be crispy. (They will get crispier after removed from skillet.) Remove from skillet and drain on paper towels. Taste and add a little salt if desired.

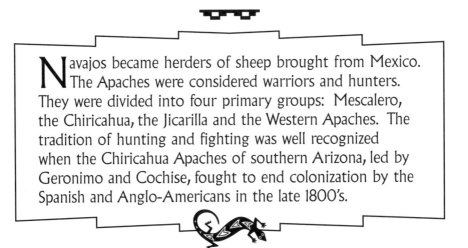

Navajos became herders of sheep brought from Mexico. The Apaches were considered warriors and hunters. They were divided into four primary groups: Mescalero, the Chiricahua, the Jicarilla and the Western Apaches. The tradition of hunting and fighting was well recognized when the Chiricahua Apaches of southern Arizona, led by Geronimo and Cochise, fought to end colonization by the Spanish and Anglo-Americans in the late 1800's.

*Fresh Tostados

1 package (12 count) corn tortillas
Oil
Salt

- Cut corn tortillas like a pizza in pie-shaped triangles. In heavy skillet or griddle with hot oil, drop tortilla triangles, turn once and fry until crispy.

- Remove from oil, drain on paper towel and sprinkle a little salt on top. Serve immediately with salsas and dips.

*Navajo Fry Bread

2 cups flour
2 teaspoons baking powder
1 teaspoon salt
⅓ cup powdered milk
¾ cup warm water
2 tablespoons lard or shortening
Oil

- In large bowl mix flour, baking powder, salt and powdered milk. Slowly pour in water and stir well. Stir and knead with hands for about 5 minutes.

- Divide into 10 to 12 balls. Melt lard and brush on outside of dough balls. Let rest for about 30 minutes. On lightly floured surface, spread each ball to about 7 to 8 inches in diameter.

- Poke hole in center and fry in 350° oil in heavy skillet until it browns lightly. Turn once and drain. Serve with butter or jam.

Southwest Spoon Bread

1 cup yellow cornmeal
1 tablespoon sugar
1 teaspoon salt
½ teaspoon baking soda
¾ cup milk
⅓ cup oil
2 eggs, beaten
1 (15 ounce) can cream-style corn
1 (4 ounce) can chopped green chiles
1 (16 ounce) package shredded cheddar cheese

- Preheat oven to 350°.

- In mixing bowl, combine and mix cornmeal, sugar, salt and baking soda. Stir in milk and oil and mix well. Add eggs and corn and mix well.

- Spoon half of batter into greased 9 x 13-inch baking dish. Sprinkle half green chiles and half cheese over batter. Repeat layers, ending with cheese. Bake uncovered for 45 minutes or until it is light brown. Serve from pan while hot.

TIP: This could be used as a substitute for potatoes or rice.

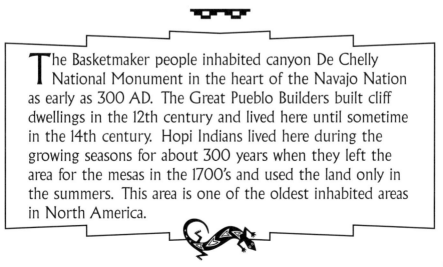

The Basketmaker people inhabited canyon De Chelly National Monument in the heart of the Navajo Nation as early as 300 AD. The Great Pueblo Builders built cliff dwellings in the 12th century and lived here until sometime in the 14th century. Hopi Indians lived here during the growing seasons for about 300 years when they left the area for the mesas in the 1700's and used the land only in the summers. This area is one of the oldest inhabited areas in North America.

*Ranch-Style Sour-Dough Starter

1 package dry yeast
2 cups flour
2 cups warm water

❦ Combine ingredients in large plastic, glass or ceramic bowl (not metal) and mix well. Cover loosely with cheesecloth or old dish towel and put in warm place for 48 hours. Stir several times each day to mix ingredients. Starter will increase in volume a little, but not the way bread rises. Store starter in refrigerator.

❦ When ready to make bread or biscuits, stir well and remove amount needed. Replenish starter with 1 cup flour and 1 cup water, mix well and store in refrigerator.

TIP: Another way to replenish sour dough starter calls for 1 cup flour, 1 cup milk and ¼ cup sugar.

Santa Fe was made the provincial capitol of the "Kingdom of New Mexico" by the Spanish in 1610. The Pueblo Indians came to the Santa Fe area around 1200 A.D., but they were preceded by the Anasazi Indians by several centuries, well before Columbus made his famous voyage.

*Round-Up Sour Dough Biscuits

1 cup flour
2 teaspoons sugar
1 teaspoon baking powder
½ teaspoon salt
¼ cup (3 tablespoons) bacon grease or butter
1 cup Ranch-Style Sour Dough Starter

👋 In large bowl, combine flour, sugar, baking powder and salt and mix well. Pour in a little bacon grease at a time and stir to mix well. Form well in center of dough and pour in sour dough starter. Stir well to mix.

👋 Lay out wax paper on counter and sprinkle flour over paper. Flour your hands and knead dough on wax paper just until smooth. Press dough out to make large piece about ½ inch thick. Use small, thin-brimmed glass and cut out biscuits.

👋 Pour a little bacon grease in 9 x 13-inch baking pan and coat bottom of pan. Place each biscuit in pan, turn them over so both sides have a little bacon grease on them. Cover with cup towel or wax paper and place in warm area for about 30 minutes.

👋 Preheat oven to 400° and bake for about 25 minutes or until biscuits are light brown. Serve hot with lots of butter and honey.

The oldest continually used highway in the U.S. is Interstate Route 25 in New Mexico. It is the same road used by Spanish explorers traveling from Mexico City to Nuevo Mexico in the 1500's. It was called the Camino Real de Tierra Adentro, "The Royal Road to the Inner Land".

81

*Easy Cinnamon Crisps

Flour tortillas
Vegetable oil
Sugar
Ground cinnamon

 Cut tortillas into wedges and carefully place in large skillet with hot oil. Fry until golden brown, remove from skillet and drain on paper towels. Sprinkle both sides of tortilla wedges heavily with sugar and cinnamon.

*Quick and Easy Sopaipillas

1 cup flour
1 cup biscuit mix
¾ cup warm water

 Mix flour and biscuit mix and slowly pour in warm water. Blend well and knead until dough is easy to handle. Divide dough into 8 balls, flatten into pancakes about ½ inch thick and cut each into 4 pieces. Let dough rest for about 5 minutes.

 Heat oil in deep fryer to about 350° and place each piece into hot oil. Deep fry, turning once, until golden brown. Pieces will puff up and be hollow. Drain and serve with honey.

*Sopaipillas

Sopaipillas are puffy, deep-fried, "pillows" of dough, traditionally served with honey.

4 cups flour
1 tablespoon sugar
1 tablespoon baking powder
2 teaspoons salt
3 tablespoons shortening
1 cup water, divided
Powdered sugar
Oil
Honey

In large bowl mix flour, baking powder, salt and sugar. Cut in shortening, stir and add just enough water to make doughy. Let stand for 15 minutes.

Layout wax paper on counter, spread powdered sugar lightly on surface and roll out dough to about ¼-inch thickness. Cut into 3-inch squares.

Heat oil in deep-fryer, drop squares into oil and cook until golden brown. Drain on paper towels. Serve with honey.

TIP: *Sopaipillas may also be rolled in mixture of ½ cup sugar mixed with 1 teaspoon cinnamon.*

Mesa Verde National Park was home to the Ancestral Puebloan people for more than 700 years. These cliff dwellings carved out of sandstone canyons and mesas offer one of the most extensive and elaborate examples of life as far back as 550 A.D. in existence.

*Bunuelos

3 cups flour, sifted
1 teaspoon baking powder
1 teaspoon salt
2 tablespoons sugar
½ cup (1 stick) butter, softened
2 eggs
¾ cup milk
Oil for frying

TOPPING:
1 cup sugar
1 teaspoon cinnamon

In large bowl, mix flour, baking powder, salt and sugar.
Cut butter into dry ingredients. Add and mix in eggs and
milk.

Knead dough until it is very smooth. Shape into 20 to 25
balls. Cover and let stand for 30 minutes.

Heat oil 2 inches deep in large saucepan or deep fryer. Roll
each ball out on lightly floured board into very thin, 6-inch
circles and cut into wedges.

Fry only a few at a time until golden brown and turn once.
Drain on paper towels. Sprinkle with sugar-cinnamon
topping while still warm.

SALADS, SOUPS & STEWS

Avocado Halves

6 ripe avocados
Lemon
Lettuce
1 tablespoon oil
1 tablespoon balsamic vinegar
Salt
½ to 1 cup shredded Mexican 4-cheese blend

🖐 Peel avocados, remove seeds and cut in half lengthwise. Sprinkle each half with a little lemon juice. Place each avocado half on bed of lettuce.

🖐 In separate bowl, mix oil and vinegar and pour a little into each avocado cavity. Lightly sprinkle salt and place shredded cheese on top to serve.

*Sonoran Tomatillo-Guacamole

Tomatillos take the place of tomatoes and give this guacamole a hint of something exotic.

3 very ripe avocados, pitted, peeled
4 or 5 fresh or canned tomatillos, drained
¼ cup minced onion
2 tablespoons canned, diced green chiles
2 tablespoons lime juice
¼ cup minced fresh cilantro
Hot sauce to taste
½ teaspoon salt
Lettuce

🖐 In medium bowl mash avocado with fork and leave a few lumps of avocado. Stir in tomatillos, onion, green chiles, lime juice, cilantro, hot sauce and salt. Cover and chill. Serve on bed of lettuce.

Surprise Avocado Salad

8 to 10 slices Canadian bacon, diced
3 to 4 ripe avocados
1 small, fresh lime
¾ cup mayonnaise
2 cloves garlic, crushed
1 teaspoon salt
½ teaspoon pepper
1½ cups frozen, cooked shrimp, thawed, chopped
Iceberg lettuce

- Fry Canadian bacon or diced ham crisp in skillet, drain and set aside. Halve avocados, remove seeds, scoop out flesh and put in small bowl, but keep outside peel as shell.

- Mash avocado flesh until smooth, add juice of lime and stir. Add mayonnaise, garlic, salt and pepper and mix well.

- Add shrimp, stir and scoop into avocado shells. Place on bed of lettuce leaves on serving plates. Sprinkle bacon over top and serve with chips.

TIP: If you do not want to fry Canadian bacon, use cooked, diced ham instead and save time.

Some of the oldest Indian artifacts found anywhere were discovered near Clovis, New Mexico and date back more than 10,000 years to the last Ice Age.

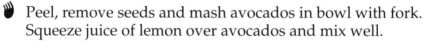
*Classic Guacamole

Traditional guacamole is mashed with a fork to get the right chunky texture. It is simple, fresh and unbelievably good.

4 to 5 ripe avocados
1 lemon
1 tomato, peeled, seeded, diced, drained
2 green onions with tops, minced
½ to 1 teaspoon minced garlic

 Peel, remove seeds and mash avocados in bowl with fork. Squeeze juice of lemon over avocados and mix well.

 Add diced tomato, green onions and garlic and mix thoroughly. Serve on bed of lettuce as individual salads or with chips as an appetizer.

Guacamole Olé

5 or 6 ripe avocados
2 green onions with tops, minced
1 tomato, seeded, minced
1 teaspoon salt
3 tablespoons lemon juice
3 tablespoons mayonnaise
1 teaspoon salad oil
1 (4 ounce) can chopped green chiles
¼ cup hot salsa
Chopped lettuce

 Peel, seed and mash avocados in medium bowl. Add onions, tomato, salt, lemon juice, mayonnaise, oil, chiles and salsa and mix well.

 Serve on bed of chopped lettuce.

Desert Flower Guacamole Ring

Lemon
3½ cups mashed avocado
2 (1 ounce) envelopes unflavored gelatin
½ cup cold water
1 cup boiling water
6 tablespoons lemon juice
¼ cup finely minced onion
4 fresh or canned tomatillos, diced
2 teaspoons salt
Scant ⅛ teaspoon hot sauce
¾ cup mayonnaise
Cherry tomatoes or fresh tomatillos

🖐 Sprinkle lemon on mashed avocado, cover and chill. Soften gelatin in cold water and stir into boiling water.

🖐 Add lemon juice, onion, 4 tomatillos, salt and hot sauce and set aside to cool.

🖐 Stir in avocado and mayonnaise. Pour into 10-inch ring mold and chill until firm. To serve, place ring on bed of lettuce with tomatoes or tomatillos in center of ring.

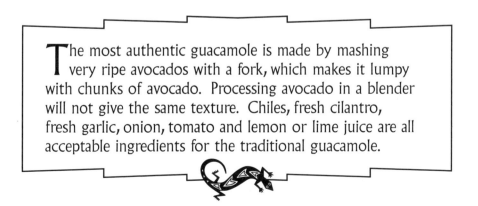

The most authentic guacamole is made by mashing very ripe avocados with a fork, which makes it lumpy with chunks of avocado. Processing avocado in a blender will not give the same texture. Chiles, fresh cilantro, fresh garlic, onion, tomato and lemon or lime juice are all acceptable ingredients for the traditional guacamole.

89

✧Refried Beans-Avocado Mix

1 (15 ounce) can refried beans
4 ounces sour cream
⅓ cup mayonnaise
3 avocados
1 lemon
2 tomatoes, diced
4 green onions with tops, chopped
2 (4 ounce) cans diced green chiles
1 clove garlic, minced
1 (10 ounce) jar hot salsa
1 (8 ounce) package shredded Monterey Jack cheese

☙ Combine refried beans, sour cream and mayonnaise and process in blender. Peel, remove seeds and mash avocados in small bowl. Squeeze juice of lemon and mix thoroughly.

☙ Add tomatoes, green onions, green chiles and garlic to avocados and stir well. Pour refried bean layer in bottom of 9-inch glass pie plate or make about a 9-inch circle in middle of large platter.

☙ Spread avocados evenly over top of beans. Pour hot salsa evenly over avocados and top with cheese. Serve with chips or crackers.

Montezuma Castle National Monument preserves the pueblo remains of the Sinagua people dating from the 1100's. The cliff dwelling is built into limestone cliffs high above Beaver Creek in Arizona.

Tomahawk Chop

1 head iceberg lettuce
1 (15 ounce) can pinto beans, drained
1 (8 ounce) package shredded cheddar cheese
1 (4 ounce) can diced green chiles, drained well
1 (14 ounce) can chopped black olives, drained
2 tomatoes, peeled, chopped
2 avocados
8 ounces tortilla chips, crushed
1 (8 ounce) bottle prepared oil and vinegar dressing, divided

🖐 Chop or tear lettuce into small pieces and place in large bowl. Add beans, cheese, green chiles, black olives and chopped tomatoes and toss lightly.

🖐 Peel, seed and chop avocados. Add avocados, tortilla chips and dressing to salad and toss gently. Serve immediately.

*Black Bean-Corn Salad

2 (15 ounce) cans whole kernel corn, drained
2 (15 ounce) cans black beans, rinsed, drained
1 large sweet red bell pepper, jullienned
1 bunch fresh green onions, sliced in 1-inch pieces
1 jalapeno chile, seeded, finely chopped
Prepared roasted garlic-vinaigrette salad dressing

🖐 In large bowl, combine corn, beans, bell pepper, onions and chile and mix well. Pour enough vinaigrette dressing over vegetables just to partially cover and stir well.

🖐 Cover and chill. Stir 2 or 3 times before serving.

Tucson Toss

1 head iceberg lettuce
1 (15 ounce) can red kidney beans, drained
1 (8 ounce) can pitted, chopped, black olives, drained
2 (4 ounce) cans chopped green chiles
3 tomatoes, chopped, drained
3 green onions with tops, chopped
2 ripe avocados
1 lemon
½ cup sour cream
2 tablespoons Italian dressing
1 teaspoon chile powder
1 teaspoon salt
¼ teaspoon pepper
1 (8 ounce) package shredded longhorn cheese
1 cup crushed tortilla chips

In large salad bowl tear lettuce into small pieces. Pour kidney beans, black olives, green chiles, tomatoes and onion on lettuce and toss.

Peel, remove seed and mash avocados. Squeeze a little lemon juice on avocados and stir. In small bowl combine sour cream, dressing, chile powder, salt and pepper and mix well.

Pour over lettuce mixture and toss to coat vegetables. Serve individual servings and top with cheese and crushed tortilla chips.

Mesa Verde Bean Salad With Nopalitos

This is really a tasty salad that is different.

1 (15 ounce) can green lima beans, drained
1 (15 ounce) can garbanzo beans, drained
1 (15 ounce) can kidney beans, drained
1 cup canned nopalitos, drained
1 cup sliced celery
4 green onions with tops, sliced
¼ cup chopped parsley

DRESSING:
½ cup olive oil
½ cup red wine vinegar
1 teaspoon grated lemon peel
1 tablespoon lemon juice
3 tablespoons sugar
1½ teaspoons salt
½ teaspoon paprika
1½ teaspoons pepper

Combine drained beans, nopalitos, celery, green onions and parsley in large bowl with lid. For dressing, mix all ingredients and blend well.

Pour over bean mixture and toss gently until vegetables are well coated. Cover and chill overnight.

TIP: Nopalitos are diced leaves of the prickly pear cactus and taste a little like pickled green beans.

93

Ensalata Especial

1 (16 ounce) can black beans, rinsed, drained
1 (8 ounce) can whole kernel corn
1 cup cooked rice
1 bunch green onions with tops, chopped
1 tomato, peeled, seeded, diced
½ red bell pepper, chopped
½ yellow bell pepper, chopped
Romaine lettuce

DRESSING:
⅓ cup olive oil
1 tablespoon sugar
¼ cup hot salsa
2 tablespoons red wine vinegar
2 cloves garlic, crushed
1 teaspoon ground cumin
1 teaspoon salt
½ teaspoon black pepper

Combine beans, corn, rice, onions, tomato and bell peppers and mix well. In small bowl, combine and mix olive oil, sugar, hot salsa, red wine vinegar, garlic, cumin, salt and pepper. Pour over vegetables and toss.

Cover and chill several hours before serving on bed of lettuce.

Saguaro (sa wah ro) cactus is the largest species of cactus in the U.S. and is unique to the Sonora Desert to the east and west of Tucson. It can live to be 200 years old and can reach heights up to 50 feet. The saguaro cactus is one of the most striking features of the American Southwest.

Taos Tomato-Garbanzo Salad

2 (15 ounce) cans garbanzo beans, drained, rinsed
1 (8 ounce) package shredded cheddar cheese
4 tomatoes, seeded, chopped
4 green onions with tops, chopped
1 bell pepper, seeded, sliced
4 lemons
⅓ cup olive oil
1 teaspoon cumin
¼ teaspoon cayenne pepper

💧 In large bowl, combine garbanzo beans, cheese, tomatoes, green onions, radishes and bell pepper and toss.

💧 In small bowl, combine juice of lemons, olive oil, salt, cumin and cayenne pepper. Pour over garbanzo mixture and toss gently. Chill before serving.

River Wash Black Beans

⅓ cup red wine vinegar
⅓ cup olive oil
2 tablespoons sugar
3 cloves garlic, crushed
3 (15 ounce) cans black beans, rinsed, drained
1 (8 ounce) can whole kernel corn
1 red bell pepper, chopped
1 purple onion, chopped

💧 Combine and mix vinegar, oil, sugar, salt and pepper. Place black beans, corn, bell pepper and onion in bowl with lid. Pour dressing over bean mixture and toss. Cover and chill several hours or overnight.

Juarez Walnut Salad

DRESSING:
¾ cup sour cream
3 tablespoons lemon juice
2 tablespoons sugar
⅓ cup olive oil
½ teaspoon seasoned salt
½ teaspoon white pepper

2 (16 ounce) whole kernel corn, drained
1 cup chopped walnuts
1 (4 ounce) can chopped green chiles
1 bell pepper, chopped
Lettuce

In small bowl, combine all dressing ingredients and mix well. Place corn, walnuts, green chiles and bell pepper in container with lid.

Pour dressing over corn mixture and toss lightly. Chill and serve over bed of lettuce.

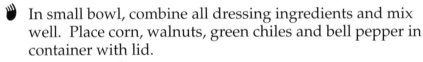

Paleo-Indians lived in southern Utah 12,000 years ago. Ancestral Puebloan people built cliff dwellings in the first century along the San Juan River and Mormons settled the area in 1847.

Crisp Cayenne Cucumbers

½ cup sugar
½ cup white vinegar
½ cup ice water
½ teaspoon salt
½ teaspoon cayenne pepper
3 seedless cucumbers, sliced
1 red onion, thinly sliced
Fresh cilantro leaves

- Combine sugar, vinegar, water, salt and cayenne pepper and set aside.

- In bowl with lid, place cucumbers and onion. Add vinegar mixture and toss. Cover and chill several hours or overnight and stir occasionally.

- To serve, drain cucumbers and onions into serving bowl and garnish with cilantro.

The Spanish, under the command of conquistador Francisco Vasquez de Coronado, headed north from Mexico City to discover the fabled Seven Cities of Cibola with streets paved in gold. In 1540 this expedition was the first to meet tribes of Indians and to see the pueblo dwellings along the Rio Grande River. This new land came to be known as "Nuevo Mexico". Coronado returned to Mexico without finding cities of gold and left this new land to Franciscan monks for the rest of the 16th century.

*Mexican Corn Salad

3 (11 ounce) cans Mexican corn with red and green bell
 peppers, drained
1 cup chopped celery
½ cup minced onion
1 (4 ounce) can chopped green chiles, drained
2 tablespoons vinegar
2 tablespoons sugar
½ teaspoon seasoning salt
¼ teaspoon white pepper
¼ teaspoon cayenne pepper

In large bowl mix corn, celery, onion and green chiles. In
separate bowl mix vinegar, sugar, salt, white pepper and
cayenne pepper and pour over corn mixture.

Mix well, chill, stir several times and serve.

Roasted Garlic-Broccoli Salad

3 cups fresh broccoli florets
1 medium jicama, julienned
1 large sweet red bell pepper, julienned
1 (11 ounce) can Mexicorn, drained
1 bunch fresh green onion, sliced
1 (15 ounce) can kidney beans, rinsed, drained, optional
Prepared roasted garlic-vinaigrette dressing

In large bowl, combine broccoli, jicama, bell pepper, corn,
onion and kidney beans. Pour dressing over vegetables
and toss to coat.

Cover and chill at least 3 hours. Toss again before serving.

Crunchy Sweet Onion-Jicama Salad

1 Supersweet 1015 onion, thinly sliced
1 medium jicama, peeled, julienned
Prepared roasted garlic-vinaigrette salad dressing
Red leaf lettuce

In bowl, place sliced onion and cover with lightly salted water. Soak for about 2 hours. Drain onion and pat dry.

Combine onions and jicama in large bowl, pour enough salad dressing to partially cover. Toss and chill.

Arrange lettuce leaves on individual salad plates and mound onion-jicama mixture onto lettuce.

Kickin' Jicama Salad

1 (1 pound) jicama, peeled
1 cup thinly sliced red onion
1 small cucumber, unpeeled, sliced
5 tomatillos, husks removed, washed, sliced
Balsamic vinaigrette dressing
¼ teaspoon hot sauce

Slice jicama in ⅛-inch slices and cut each slice into ⅛-inch strips. Place in large container with lid, add red onion, cucumber and tomatillos and toss lightly to mix.

Pour small amount of dressing and hot sauce over salad, toss to determine correct amount of dressing. Add dressing if needed, toss and chill for 1 to 2 hours. Toss again before serving. Use slotted spoon to remove salad from container and serve in lettuce-lined salad bowl.

Cimarron Slaw

2 cups finely shredded green cabbage
2 cups finely shredded red cabbage
1 cup jicama julienne
¼ cup diced green bell pepper
¼ cup thinly sliced green onions with tops
½ cup chopped, fresh cilantro leaves

DRESSING:
¼ cup oil
1 tablespoon sugar
¼ cup lime juice
¾ teaspoon salt
¼ teaspoon black pepper
½ cup sour cream

Combine and mix cabbages, jicama, bell pepper, green onions and cilantro in large bowl.

For dressing, mix oil, sugar, lime juice, salt, black pepper and sour cream and blend well. Pour over cabbage mixture and toss lightly. Cover and chill 3 to 6 hours for flavors to blend.

The history of the U.S. really began 80 years before the Pilgrims landed at Plymouth Rock. In 1540 Spanish conquistadors were exploring Nuevo Mexico establishing Spanish dominance in the region. Their influence is still felt today in the food, architecture, language and traditions.

Chicken Salad In Avocado Boats

6 to 8 boneless, skinless, chicken breast halves, cooked
1 cup chopped celery
3 hard-boiled eggs, chopped
½ cup chopped pecans
1 cup mayonnaise
Salt
Pepper
6 to 8 ripe avocados
Fresh lemon juice
Iceberg lettuce
12 to 16 grape tomatoes
Paprika

Chop chicken into small pieces and gently fold in celery, hard-boiled eggs, pecans, mayonnaise and salt and pepper to taste. Cut avocados in half lengthwise, remove seed and sprinkle with lemon juice. (Do not peel.)

Place avocados on lettuce, scoop chicken salad into cavity of avocados, slice grape tomatoes in half lengthwise and place around avocados. Sprinkle with paprika and serve immediately.

Athabascans, a nomadic people who migrated from the far north down the Rocky Mountains to the south, became the Navajo and Apache nations in the early part of the 15th century, before Columbus discovered the new world.

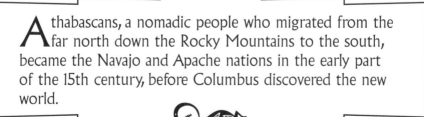

101

Santa Fe Chicken-Pasta Salad

6 boneless, skinless chicken breast halves, cooked
2 cloves garlic, finely minced
3 tablespoons olive oil
2 tablespoons white wine vinegar
1 teaspoon sugar
2 zucchini
1 pound fettucini, cooked, rinsed, cooled
1 (16 ounce) can garbanzo beans
1 bunch green onions with tops, chopped
2 bunches fresh cilantro, chopped
2 jalapeno peppers, seeded, minced
2 tomatoes, chopped, drained
½ cup sour cream
1 (3 ounce) cream cheese, softened
1½ teaspoons ground cumin
1 teaspoon salt
½ teaspoon pepper

Cut chicken into bite-size pieces. Combine and mix garlic, oil, vinegar and sugar. Cut zucchini into match-stick pieces and saute in a little butter or oil.

In large bowl, combine fettucini, zucchini, garbanzo beans, onions, cilantro, jalapeno peppers, tomatoes, sour cream, cream cheese, cumin, salt and pepper and mix well.

Add chicken and oil mixture and toss. Chill at least 1 hour before serving.

Shrimp Coriander

30 to 36 small to medium, cooked shrimp, peeled, veined
3 medium tomatoes, chopped
2 avocados, peeled, cubed
1 (4 ounce) can chopped green chiles
2 ribs celery, sliced
3 tablespoons finely chopped coriander leaves
Lettuce

DRESSING:
3 tablespoons olive oil
2 teaspoons sugar
1 teaspoon salt
½ cup lime juice

- Combine and mix shrimp, tomatoes, avocados, green chiles, celery and coriander leaves.

- Quickly mix oil, sugar, salt and lime juice and pour over shrimp mixture. (Do this quickly so avocados will not darken.) Toss together and chill. Serve on bed of lettuce.

Native American Indians, descendents of ancient nomadic and agricultural tribes who built the elaborate cliff dwellings of the Southwest, preceded Spanish explorers by hundreds of years. Evidence dating as far back as 800 A.D. gives evidence of the strong hold Indian tribes had on the region. Today, their influence is seen in the region's food, architecture, native Indian languages, religious customs and traditional ways.

103

*Taco Salad Supper

2 pounds lean ground beef
1 head lettuce
1 (15 ounce) can pinto beans, drained
2 tomatoes, seeded, chopped
5 to 6 green onions with tops, chopped
1 (4 ounce) can chopped green chiles, drained
Salt and pepper
2 tablespoons cumin
1 (8 ounce) package shredded cheddar cheese
1 (8 ounce) jar spicy salsa
Tortilla chips

In large skillet brown ground beef, drain and set aside.
Tear lettuce into small pieces and put in large bowl. Make
a well in middle of lettuce and place ground beef.

Put beans, tomatoes, green onions, chopped green chiles,
salt, pepper and cumin in separate bowl and stir well.
Spoon over ground beef.

Sprinkle cheese on top and serve with salsa for dressing
and chips.

The largest group of petroglyphs in the Southwest may
be viewed at the Petroglyphs National Monument west
of Albuquerque. More than 25,000 images were carved
into rock surfaces as many as 1000 years ago.

Fiesta Taco Salad

1 pound ground beef
1 (8 ounce) jar hot salsa, divided
½ teaspoon crushed oregano
½ teaspoon salt

DRESSING:
½ cup sour cream
½ cup French or ranch dressing

1 (15 ounce) can kidney beans, drained
1 (2 ounce) can sliced, pitted ripe olives, drained
¾ medium head iceberg lettuce, shredded
2 tomatoes, diced
½ red onion, chopped
1 (8 ounce) shredded cheddar cheese
1 avocado
1 teaspoon cumin seeds
1 (16 ounce) bag tortilla chips

❧ Crumble meat into large skillet, stir over medium heat until meat browns and drain. Add ½ cup salsa, oregano and salt and cook 2 minutes, stirring constantly.

❧ To make dressing, whisk sour cream, French dressing and ½ cup salsa in small bowl until it blends well. When ready to serve, combine meat mixture, beans, olives, lettuce, tomatoes, onion and cheese.

❧ Peel, seed and chop avocado and add to salad. Pour dressing over salad and sprinkle with cumin seeds. Toss gently to mix.

❧ Place 6 to 8 tortilla chips on each serving plate and top with salad. Serve immediately with additional tortilla chips.

Rio Grande Gazpacho

This spicy vegetable soup made from a puree of raw vegetables is served cold and is great in the summer.

1 cucumber, peeled, seeded, quartered
1 bell pepper, seeded, quartered
½ onion, quartered
1 clove garlic, minced
2 teaspoons chopped parsley
3¼ cups tomato juice, divided
1 pound tomatoes, peeled, quartered, cored
¼ cup sliced pimento-stuffed olives
3 tablespoons red wine vinegar
1 tablespoon olive oil
½ teaspoon salt
½ teaspoon cumin
½ teaspoon oregano
⅛ teaspoon hot sauce

Combine cucumber, bell pepper, onion, garlic, parsley and 2 cups tomato juice in blender. Process until vegetables are coarsely chopped. Add tomatoes and process again until vegetables are finely chopped.

Pour into medium container with tight lid. Stir in olives, wine vinegar, oil, salt, cumin, oregano and hot sauce.

Stir in remaining tomato juice, cover and chill about 24 hours. Serve cold in individual bowls.

White Gazpacho

¼ cup packed parsley leaves
3 cloves garlic, chopped
1 teaspoon dried basil leaves
1 teaspoon dried oregano leaves
3 seedless cucumbers, chopped
1 green bell pepper, seeded, quartered
1 white onion, quartered
4 green onions with tops, chopped
2 (8 ounce) cartons plain yogurt
2 (14 ounce) cans chicken broth
2 tablespoons lemon juice
½ teaspoon salt
½ teaspoon white pepper
Hot sauce
Sliced ripe olives

- In blender, finely chop parsley, garlic, basil and oregano. Add cucumbers, green pepper and onions and process until coarsely chopped.

- Blend in yogurt, broth, lemon juice and salt and mix well. Season to taste with hot sauce and chill. Serve cold garnished with sliced, ripe olives.

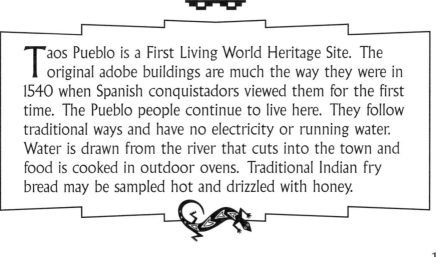

Taos Pueblo is a First Living World Heritage Site. The original adobe buildings are much the way they were in 1540 when Spanish conquistadors viewed them for the first time. The Pueblo people continue to live here. They follow traditional ways and have no electricity or running water. Water is drawn from the river that cuts into the town and food is cooked in outdoor ovens. Traditional Indian fry bread may be sampled hot and drizzled with honey.

Cream of Jalapeno Soup

3 carrots, peeled, diced
2 ribs celery, chopped
1 green bell pepper, seeded, chopped
6 tablespoons (¾ stick) butter, divided
2 (14 ounce) cans chicken broth
3 cups shredded, cooked chicken
3 to 5 jalapenos, seeded, chopped
¼ cup flour
1½ teaspoons ground cumin
1 pint whipping cream

Combine carrots, celery and bell pepper in large skillet and saute in 4 tablespoons (½ stick) butter. Transfer to large soup pot or kettle and add chicken broth, shredded chicken and jalapenos (3 for medium heat and 5 for serious heat). Bring to a boil, reduce heat and simmer for about 30 minutes.

In same skillet, melt remaining 2 tablespoons and add flour and cumin. Heat mixture on low to medium heat, stirring constantly, to make roux, but do not brown. Stir in whipping cream, stirring constantly, but do not boil.

Pour cream mixture into vegetable-chicken mixture and heat on medium just until mixture thickens.

When handling chile peppers, it is always best to wear gloves or to wash hands, knife and cutting board with soap and water after handling. Never rub your eyes after handling chili peppers.

*Corn Soup Olé

2 (15 ounce) cans whole kernel corn
½ onion, chopped
2 tablespoons (¼ stick) butter
2 tablespoons flour
½ teaspoon salt
¼ teaspoon black pepper
1 (14 ounce) can chicken broth
1½ cups half-and-half cream
1 (8 ounce) package shredded cheddar cheese
1 (4 ounce) can chopped green chiles
Tortilla chips
Bacon bits

Saute corn and onion in butter. Add flour, salt and pepper and cook 1 minute. Gradually add broth and half-and-half while on low to medium heat. Cook until it thickens slightly.

Add cheddar cheese and green chiles. Heat but do not boil. Serve soup in individual bowls and stir in 4 to 5 crumbled, tortilla chips. Garnish with bacon bits.

The oldest continually operated church in the U.S. was built by the Tlaxcala people from Mexico City and was named San Miguel Mission. It is located on the Old Santa Fe Trail in New Mexico.

*Green Chile-Corn Chowder

¼ pound bacon
1 medium onion, minced
1 (15 ounce) can whole kernel corn with liquid
1 (15 ounce) can Mexican-style diced, stewed tomatoes
2 to 3 fesh green chiles, roasted, peeled, seeded, chopped
2 large baking potatoes
1 teaspoon sugar
½ teaspoon salt
1 teaspoon paprika
¼ teaspoon white pepper
3 cups boiling water
1 (5 ounce) can evaporated milk

- Cut bacon into very small pieces and fry to crisp in skillet. Add onion and cook until translucent. Transfer to soup pot.

- Add corn with liquid, tomatoes, chiles, potatoes, sugar and seasonings and cook on low to medium until potatoes are tender. Remove from heat and slowly stir in evaporated milk. Serve immediately.

Archaeological digs in Las Vegas, New Mexico show signs of Paleo Indians living in the area as early as 8000 B.C.

✴Green Chile Soup

5 slices bacon, cut into 1-inch pieces, divided
1 onion, finely chopped
2 ribs celery, finely chopped
3 potatoes, peeled, cubed
1 (7 ounce) can chopped green chiles
2 (14 ounce) cans chicken broth
½ cup water
½ teaspoon seasoned salt
½ teaspoon white pepper
1 pint half-and-half cream

💧 In stew pot or kettle, fry bacon pieces until half done. Put half the bacon in separate bowl and set aside. Add onion and celery to stew pot and cook on medium heat until onion is translucent.

💧 Add potatoes, green chiles, chicken broth, water, seasoned salt and pepper. Cook on low to medium heat until potatoes are tender, about 15 minutes. To make soup a little thicker, mash some potatoes with fork against sides of pan.

💧 When ready to serve, pour in cream and heat, but do not return to boil. Microwave remaining bacon until crisp. Sprinkle a spoonful of crumbled bacon on top of each serving to garnish.

S mall chiles are usually hotter than large chiles.

Creamy Chile-Cheese Soup

½ onion, minced
1 large tomato, minced
1 large, fresh green chile, peeled, seeded, minced
½ clove garlic, minced
3 tablespoons butter, divided
1 (10 ounce) can chicken broth
2 tablespoons flour
3 cups milk, divided
½ teaspoon salt
¼ teaspoon white pepper
1 (12 ounce) package shredded Monterey Jack cheese

❦ Saute onion, tomato, green chile and garlic until translucent in large skillet with 1 tablespoon butter. Pour in chicken stock, stir gently and pour into large saucepan.

❦ In skillet, melt 2 tablespoons butter, add flour and stir constantly until mixture is smooth and beige in color. Stir out any lumps.

❦ Slowly pour in 1½ cups milk and stir constantly until sauce thickens slightly. Pour mixture into saucepan and continue cooking on simmer.

❦ Pour in remaining milk, salt, white pepper and cheese into saucepan and stir constantly. Simmer until cheese melts. Pour into soup cups and serve immediately.

Red chiles are usually riper and milder than green ones of the same variety.

*Chile-Frijole Soup

1½ pounds pinto beans
5 slices thick-sliced bacon, cut in pieces
2 onions, chopped
1 teaspoon garlic powder
½ teaspoon black pepper
½ teaspoon ground thyme
½ teaspoon ground oregano
½ teaspoon cayenne pepper
1 tablespoon salt

- Wash beans, place in large soup pot or kettle and cover with water. Soak overnight and drain.

- In skillet cook bacon and onions for about 5 minutes. Transfer with pan drippings to soup pot. Bring to boil and add all seasonings except salt.

- Lower heat and cook 4 hours. Add hot water when liquid goes below original level. When beans are done, remove about half of beans.

- Mash beans with potato masher or process them in blender. Return to pot and add salt. Serve hot with hot flour tortillas and butter.

Spotted pinto beans is the traditional variety of beans eaten in the Southwest. They are used for frijole dishes and refritos or refried beans.

Spicy Bean Soup

1 (15 ounce) can refried beans
1 (14 ounce) can chicken broth
2 (4 ounce) cans chopped green chiles
2 cloves garlic, minced
2 to 3 jalapeno chiles, seeded, chopped
¼ teaspoon black pepper
1 teaspoon chile powder
6 slices bacon
1 bunch green onions with tops, chopped, divided
5 ribs celery, chopped
1 bell pepper, seeded, chopped
1 (8 ounce) package shredded cheddar cheese

❂ In large saucepan, heat refried beans and chicken broth and whisk beans and broth together. Add green chiles, garlic, jalapenos, black pepper and chile powder and stir well. Reduce heat to low and stir occasionally.

❂ In skillet fry bacon until crisp and in pan drippings saute with about ¾ onions, celery and bell peppers until onions are translucent.

❂ Crumble bacon and put into bean soup. Add onions, celery, bell peppers and pan drippings and stir well. Bring to boil, reduce heat to low and serve immediately.

❂ Garnish with remaining onions and cheese.

Cowboy Sausage-Bean Soup

1 pound pork sausage
2 (15 ounce) cans pinto beans
2 (15 ounce) cans stewed tomatoes
1 quart water
1 onion, chopped
1 teaspoon seasoning salt
¼ teaspoon garlic powder
½ teaspoon thyme
1 tablespoon chile powder
¼ teaspoon ground coriander
¼ teaspoon black pepper
1 large potato, peeled, diced
1 bell pepper, chopped
1 (8 ounce) package cubed processed cheese
½ cup grated Monterey Jack cheese

- In large Dutch oven, brown sausage and drain fat. Add beans, tomatoes, water, onions, seasoning salt, garlic powder, thyme, chile powder, coriander and black pepper.

- Bring to boil, turn heat down and cover. Simmer for 1 hour. Add potatoes and bell pepper, cover and simmer another 30 minutes or until potatoes are soft, but not mushy.

- Stir in cheese and heat just until it melts. To serve, sprinkle each serving with Monterey Jack cheese.

Billy the Kid was shot to death by Sheriff Pat Garrett on a ranch outside of Fort Sumner, New Mexico in 1881.

Black Bart's Black Bean Soup

Black beans are small but pack a hearty flavor.

2 cups dried black beans
2 to 3 cups diced ham
1 onion, chopped
1 carrot, chopped
2 ribs celery, chopped
3 jalapeno chiles, seeded, chopped
2 (14 ounce) cans chicken broth
4 cups water
2 teaspoons cumin
1 teaspoon salt
2 tablespoons snipped fresh cilantro
½ teaspoon oregano
1 teaspoon chile powder
⅛ teaspoon cayenne pepper
1 (8 ounce) carton sour cream

 Wash black beans and soak in water overnight. Drain beans and pour into heavy soup pot. Place all ingredients except sour cream in soup pot.

Bring to boil, turn heat down and simmer for about 3 hours or until beans are tender. Stir occasionally and add more water if needed for liquid to have thin, soup consistency.

Place a few cups at a time in food processor or blender and puree until it is smooth. Add sour cream and reheat soup, but do not boil. Serve in individual bowls.

TIP: *If you want a quick version of this soup, substitute 3 (15 ounce) cans black beans, rinsed and drained, for dried beans.*

Ranchero Black Bean Soup

1 cup dried black beans
3 (14 ounce) cans beef broth
1 large bunch green onions with tops, chopped
5 ribs celery, chopped
3 cloves garlic, minced
½ cup (1 stick) butter
¼ cup olive oil
½ cup uncooked rice
1 bay leaf
6 peppercorns
1 teaspoon salt
½ teaspoon cayenne pepper

Sort beans, rinse and soak in water overnight. Drain beans, transfer to large saucepan and cook about 2 hours in beef broth. In skillet saute onions, celery and garlic in butter and oil until onions are translucent.

Transfer onions, celery, garlic, rice, bay leaf, peppercorns, salt and cayenne pepper to beans and cook another 2 hours or until beans are tender. (Add water if needed.) Remove bay leaf and peppercorns before serving.

TIP: *When serving, it is a nice touch to garnish with grated cheese, sour cream or chopped green onions on top.*

The Anasazi pueblos, located in the area where New Mexico, Arizona, Colorado and Utah come together, were the largest cities in what is now the United States for almost 200 years. Archaeologists disagree about why the pueblos were abandoned.

*Albondigas Soup

This is a traditional Southwest dish. Albondigas is Spanish for meatballs.

MEATBALLS:
1 pound ground beef
1 pound ground pork
3 eggs
1 cup dry breadcrumbs
⅓ cup milk
1 small onion, finely chopped
2 tablespoons snipped fresh cilantro
1 teaspoon salt
1 teaspoon pepper
1 teaspoon dried oregano

MEATBALLS:
🖐 Combine all meatball ingredients, form into 1-inch balls and set aside.

SOUP:
4 cups water
2 (14 ounce) cans condensed beef broth
1 cup tomato juice
1 onion, chopped
½ cup chopped celery
1 chopped carrot
1 zucchini, chopped
1 jalapeno pepper, seeded, chopped
½ teaspoon salt
½ teaspoon pepper
1 clove garlic, minced
Cilantro sprigs

SOUP:
🖐 Combine water, beef broth, tomato juice, onion, celery, carrot and meatballs in large roaster. Bring to boil, reduce heat and simmer, uncovered, for 20 minutes.

(Continued on next page.)

(Continued)

🖐 Add zucchini, jalapeno, salt, pepper and garlic and simmer uncovered for 20 minutes more or until vegetables are tender. Serve in individual bowls and garnish with cilantro sprigs.

Tip: Use prepared, frozen meatballs to save time.

Quick Mexican-Meatball Soup

3 (14 ounce) cans beef broth
1 (16 ounce) jar hot salsa
1 (16 ounce) package frozen whole kernel corn, thawed
1 (16 ounce) package frozen meatballs, thawed
1 teaspoon minced garlic

🖐 Combine all ingredients soup pot and stir well. Heat to boiling, reduce heat and simmer for about 45 minutes.

Easy Mexican-Beef Soup

2 pounds lean ground beef
2 (15 ounce) cans chile without beans
3 (14 ounce) cans beef broth
2 (15 ounce) cans Mexican-stewed tomatoes
2 (4 ounce) cans diced green chiles
1 teaspoon seasoned salt

🖐 In skillet, brown ground beef until no longer pink and transfer to soup pot.

🖐 Add chile, broth, stewed tomatoes, green chiles, 1 cup water, seasoned salt and stir well. Cover and cook on low to medium for about 45 minutes.

La Placita Chicken Enchilada Soup

6 to 8 boneless, skinless chicken breast halves
12 cups water
½ cup (1 stick) butter
2 cloves garlic, minced
1 onion, minced
1 teaspoon seasoned salt
1 cup flour
1 (15 ounce) can Mexican tomatoes, chopped
1 (10 ounce) can chopped green chiles
1 pint sour cream
1 (8 ounce) package shredded cheddar cheese

- Cook chicken in water until tender. Reserve broth, cube chicken and set aside. In large roasting pan melt butter and cook garlic and onion until tender.

- Add seasoned salt to flour, slowly stir in flour and stir constantly to dissolve all lumps. Continue stirring and slowly pour in reserved chicken broth. Cook until soup thickens to right consistency.

- Add chicken, tomatoes, green chiles and sour cream. Mix well and heat. Serve in individual bowls and sprinkle with cheese.

True Southwest cooking is a mixture of American Indian, Spanish and Anglo-American cultures and foods. For more than 500 years Southwest cooking stands as a very consistent regional cuisine. It continues to rely heavily on its distinguishing ingredient, chile peppers.

Quick Enchilada Soup

1 pound lean ground beef, browned, drained
1 (15 ounce) can Mexican stewed tomatoes
2 (15 ounce) cans pinto beans with liquid
1 (15 ounce) can whole kernel corn with liquid
1 onion, chopped
2 (10 ounce) cans enchilada sauce
1 (8 ounce) package shredded 4-cheese blend

Combine browned beef, tomatoes, beans, corn, onion, enchilada sauce and 1 cup water in stew pot. Bring to boil, reduce heat and simmer for 35 minutes. When serving, sprinkle a little shredded cheese over each serving.

*Cantina Taco Soup

1½ pounds lean ground beef
1 (1 ounce) envelope taco seasoning
2 (15 ounce) cans Mexican stewed tomatoes
1 (15 ounce) can whole kernel corn, drained
Crushed tortilla chips
Shredded cheddar cheese

Brown ground beef in skillet until it is no longer pink and transfer to stew pot. Add taco seasoning, tomatoes, corn and 1 cup water.

On high heat, bring to boil, reduce heat and simmer for about 35 minutes. When serving, spoon a heaping tablespoon crushed tortilla chips and heaping tablespoon cheese over each serving.

Taco-Chile Soup

2 pounds very lean stew meat
1 (154 ounce) can beef broth
2 (15 ounce) cans Mexican stewed tomatoes
1 (1 ounce) package taco seasoning mix
2 (15 ounce) cans pinto beans with liquid
1 (15 ounce) can whole kernel corn with liquid
1 (8 ounce) package cubed Mexican processed cheese

- Cut large pieces of stew meat in half and brown in large skillet.

- Combine stew meat, tomatoes, taco seasoning mix, beans, corn and ¾ cup water in stew pot. (If you are not into "spicy", use original recipe stewed tomatoes instead of Mexican.)

- Bring to boil, reduce heat and simmer for 1 hour or until meat is tender. Stir in cheese when ready to serve.

Tip: For garnish top each serving with chopped green onions.

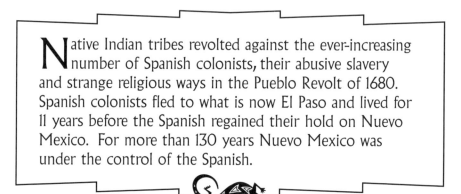

Native Indian tribes revolted against the ever-increasing number of Spanish colonists, their abusive slavery and strange religious ways in the Pueblo Revolt of 1680. Spanish colonists fled to what is now El Paso and lived for 11 years before the Spanish regained their hold on Nuevo Mexico. For more than 130 years Nuevo Mexico was under the control of the Spanish.

*Sopa De Lima

This is a traditional lime and tortilla soup.

4 to 6 boneless, skinless chicken breast halves
1 onion, minced
1 red bell pepper, seeded, chopped
2 cloves garlic, minced
2 tablespoons canola oil
6 limes, divided
3 fresh jalapeno or serrano chiles, seeded, minced
3 tomatoes, peeled, seeded, chopped
5 (14 ounce) cans chicken broth
Salt and pepper
8 corn tortillas

- Cook chicken, chop into small pieces and set aside. Cook onion, bell pepper and garlic in saucepan with hot oil until onion is translucent. Cut 1 lime in half, juice lime and place 2 shells into saucepan. Slice remaining limes and set aside.

- Add chiles, tomatoes and broth, simmer for about 10 minutes and discard lime shells. Season chicken with salt and pepper and add to saucepan.

- Cut tortillas in half and slice into narrow strips. Heat oil in large skillet and cook tortilla strips until crispy. Drain on paper towel and put in warm oven until all strips are cooked.

- Taste soup for seasonings. Pour into individual soup bowls and put lime slice and tortilla strips on top.

*Tortilla Soup Con Queso

3 (14 ounce) cans chicken broth
1 (15 ounce) can diced stewed tomatoes
4 green onions with tops, chopped
2 (4 ounce) cans diced green chiles, drained
1 clove garlic, minced
2 tablespoons oil
8 corn tortillas
1 (16 ounce) package cubed Mexican processed cheese

- In large saucepan pour chicken broth, tomatoes, onions, green chiles and garlic and heat on medium.

- Cut tortillas into long, narrow strips. In skillet with hot oil, fry tortilla strips about 10 seconds on all sides or until strips are crisp. Remove from skillet and drain.

- Heat soup to boiling, reduce heat to low and stir in cheese. Serve in individual bowls and garnish with tortilla strips.

*Fresh Avocado Soup

3 ripe avocados
4 tablespoons fresh lemon juice
1 (10 ounce) consomme
1 (8 ounce) carton plain yogurt
Salt
White pepper
Chopped chives

- Peel avocados, remove seeds and cut into pieces. Immediately put avocados, lemon juice, consomme and yogurt into blender and process until smooth. Add salt and white pepper to taste and chill several hours. Serve in soup bowls with chopped chives on top.

*Tortilla Soup

3 large boneless, skinless chicken breast halves, cooked,
    cubed
1 (10 ounce) package frozen whole kernel corn, thawed
1 onion, chopped
3 (14 ounce) cans chicken broth
2 (10 ounce) cans tomatoes and green chiles
2 teaspoons ground cumin
1 teaspoon chile powder
1 clove garlic, minced
6 corn tortillas

🖐 Preheat oven to 350°.

🖐 Combine all ingredients except tortillas in large stew pot.
    Bring to boil, reduce heat and simmer 35 minutes.

🖐 While soup is simmering, cut tortillas into 1-inch strips and
    place on baking sheet. Bake about 5 minutes or until crisp.
    Serve tortilla strips with each serving of soup.

Beans-Barley Soup

2 (15 ounce) cans pinto beans with liquid
2 (15 ounce) cans navy beans with liquid
3 (14 ounce) cans chicken broth
½ cup quick-cooking barley
1 (15 ounce) can Mexican-style stewed tomatoes
½ teaspoon black pepper

🖐 Combine all ingredients in soup pot and bring to boil.
    Reduce heat and simmer 45 minutes.

*Posole

Posole is a traditional dish made famous in Jalisco, Mexico. Families pass recipes through generations and all have opinions about the ingredients for their special dish. This recipe is a faster version than the typical all-day soups or stews.

1 pound pork boneless shoulder, cut into ½-inch pieces
¼ cup flour
¼ cup oil
1 clove garlic, minced
1 onion, chopped
1 (15 ounce) can pinto beans with liquid
1 carrot, grated
2 ribs celery, chopped
1 (7 ounce) cans chopped green chiles
½ teaspoon cayenne pepper
2 (14 ounce) cans chicken broth
1 (15 ounce) can hominy, drained
1 teaspoon salt
1½ teaspoons dried oregano leaves

 Dredge pieces of pork in flour. Heat oil in Dutch oven or kettle and brown pork on all sides. Add garlic and onion, saute until onion is translucent and drain excess oil.

 Stir in beans, carrot, celery, green chiles, cayenne pepper and chicken broth. Bring to boil, lower heat and simmer, covered, for about 45 minutes.

 Stir in hominy, salt and oregano leaves and simmer 15 to 20 minutes. Serve with hot corn tortillas.

*Quick-Step Posole

1½ to 2 pounds boneless pork shoulder, cubed
1 teaspoon salt
½ teaspoon pepper
2 tablespoons oil
¼ cup flour
2 onions, chopped
1 clove garlic, minced
2 ribs celery, chopped
1 (8 ounce) can hominy, drained
1 (10 ounce) can red chile sauce

- Season pork with salt and pepper and dredge in flour on all sides.

- Heat oil in large saucepan and brown pork pieces. Add onions, garlic and celery and cook until onions are translucent.

- Add hominy and red chile sauce to saucepan and cook on low, covered, until pork is tender. Stir occasionally. Serve with soft or crisp tortillas.

Posole is a traditional holiday dish that originated in Jalisco, Mexico and usually is served on holidays and special occasions. It is a thick soup or stew with pork (usually pork shoulder), hominy, garlic, onion, chiles and cilantro. It is served with shredded lettuce, radishes, onions as well various vegetables and herbs so each individual may create their own special dish.

Chicken and Rice Soup With Green Chiles

8 boneless, skinless chicken breast halves, cooked
2 (14 ounce) cans chicken broth
1 cup chopped celery
1 cup uncooked rice
2 to 4 large green chiles, seeded, chopped
2 teaspoons salt
¼ teaspoon white pepper

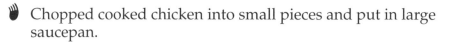 Chopped cooked chicken into small pieces and put in large saucepan.

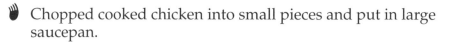 Add chicken broth, celery, rice, green chiles, salt and white pepper and simmer for about 35 minutes or until rice is tender.

Santa Fe Stew

Cornbread is a must to serve with this great stew.

1½ pounds lean ground beef
1 (14 ounce) can beef broth
1 (15 ounce) can whole kernel corn with liquid
2 (15 ounce) cans pinto beans with liquid
2 (15 ounce) cans Mexican stewed tomatoes
1 (1 ounce) envelope taco seasoning
1 (8 ounce) package cubed, processed cheese

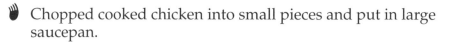 Brown beef until no longer pink in large skillet. Place in stew pot or kettle and add broth, corn, beans, stewed tomatoes, taco seasoning and ½ cup water.

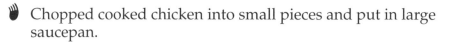 Cook on low to medium heat for 2 to 3 hours. When ready to serve, fold in cheese chunks and stir until cheese melts.

*Green Chile Stew Pot (Caldillo)

Caldillo or stew is a traditional dish served on special occasions.

2 pounds round steak, cubed
1 tablespoon seasoned salt
Canola oil
2 onions, chopped
2 potatoes, peeled, diced
2 cloves garlic, minced
6 to 8 fresh green chiles, roasted, peeled, seeded, diced
1 teaspoon salt
½ teaspoon pepper

- Sprinkle round steak with seasoned salt, heat oil in large skillet and brown meat. Put onions, potatoes, and garlic in same skillet and cook until onions are translucent.

- Pour all ingredients from skillet into large stew or soup. Add chiles, pepper and enough water to cover. Bring to boil, lower heat and simmer 1 to 2 hours until meat and potatoes are tender.

Chile peppers were known in Mexico and the New World before the Spanish explorers made their way through Mexico. While they did not find cities of gold, they did introduce the Old World to the pungent flavor and excitement of chiles. Today, more than 200 varieties of chiles exist and they are important ingredients to the cuisines of Mexico, America, Spain, South America, Africa, China and Thailand.

Cattle Drive Chile Stew

3 tablespoons canola oil
3 pounds stew meat
1 medium onion, chopped
3 ribs celery, chopped
2 carrots, chopped
1 (28 ounce) can Mexican stewed tomatoes
3 (10 ounce) cans beef broth
1 (10 ounce) package frozen whole kernel corn
1 cup diced, fresh green chiles
2 teaspoons salt
¼ teaspoon pepper

Brown stew meat on all sides in large skillet with canola oil and remove to large soup pot. In skillet drippings saute onion and celery until translucent and pour drippings and vegetables into soup pot.

Stir in tomatoes and liquid, beef broth, corn, chiles and seasonings and bring to boil. Reduce heat to low and simmer several hours.

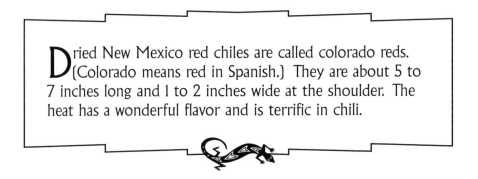

Dried New Mexico red chiles are called colorado reds. (Colorado means red in Spanish.) They are about 5 to 7 inches long and 1 to 2 inches wide at the shoulder. The heat has a wonderful flavor and is terrific in chili.

Hearty Ranch Bean Stew

½ pound lean beef stew meat
1 pound pork loin, cubed
2 tablespoons oil
Salt and pepper
1 (14 ounce) can beef broth
2 (15 ounce) cans ranch-style beans with liquid
2 (15 ounce) cans Mexican stewed tomatoes
1 (11 ounce) can Mexicorn
1 green bell pepper, chopped
1 (1 ounce) envelope ranch dressing mix
1 teaspoon ground cumin
1 ancho chile
Crushed tortilla chips

🖐 Brown beef and pork meats in hot oil in heavy stew pot or kettle; salt and pepper meats. Add beef broth and heat to boiling. Reduce heat and simmer for 30 minutes. Add beans, tomatoes, corn, bell pepper, dressing mix, cumin, ancho chile and ½ cup water; simmer for about 20 minutes.

🖐 Before serving, remove ancho. Serve in bowl with a handful of crushed chips on top of each bowl.

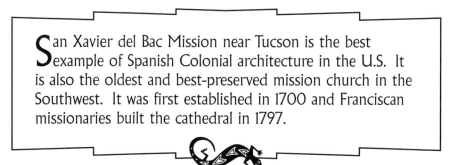

San Xavier del Bac Mission near Tucson is the best example of Spanish Colonial architecture in the U.S. It is also the oldest and best-preserved mission church in the Southwest. It was first established in 1700 and Franciscan missionaries built the cathedral in 1797.

*Chile Verde Con Carne

"Chile con carne" means chile with meat. Verde refers to the fresh green chiles.

2 to 3 pounds cubed sirloin or tenderloin
½ cup (1 stick) butter
2 onions, chopped
4 to 6 cloves garlic, minced
8 to 10 fresh whole green chiles, peeled, seeded, chopped
1 tablespoon ground cumin
2 teaspoons oregano
1 teaspoon salt
1 teaspoon black pepper
½ to 1 cup water, optional

Brown sirloin in butter in large skillet. Reduce heat to low and add all remaining ingredients. Simmer covered for about 2 to 3 hours. Stir occasionally and add water if necessary. Remove cover, taste for flavor and adjust seasonings if needed.

TIP: To save time, chile powder may be substituted instead of roasting fresh green chiles, but the flavors of fresh chiles are the secret to the best chili.

Chile or Chili?
The controversy over the spelling of chile and chili is a matter of record between people in Texas and New Mexico. Texans believe that chili spelled with an "i" is a dish. New Mexicans believe that chile with an "e" refers to the plant and the dish. Texans claim to know how to spell the dish they invented and that the dictionary agrees with them.

*Bowl of Red Chile, New Mexico-Style

This chile is what you get in New Mexico. This is also called "Chili Con Carne".

Vegetable oil
2 pounds chuck or pork roast, cubed
2 (14 ounce) cans beef broth
6 to 8 dried New Mexico red chiles, ground or 4 to 5 dried chipotle chiles, ground
4 to 6 cloves garlic, minced
3 tablespoons paprika
1 tablespoon oregano
1 teaspoon salt

Heat oil in large skillet or Dutch oven and brown meat on all sides. Add beef broth and ground chiles and bring to boil. Reduce heat, simmer about 2 and stir occasionally.

Add garlic, paprika, cumin, oregano and salt, cover and simmer another 1 hour. Stir occasionally and skim off grease.

Senator Pete Dominici of New Mexico officially stated the case for all New Mexicans in the Congressional Record in 1983. He said, "Knowing that criticizing the dictionary is akin to criticizing the Bible, I nevertheless stand here before the full Senate of the United States and with the backing of my New Mexican constituents state unequivocally, that the dictionary is wrong. Chile is spelled with an 'e'."

To signify the support of Dominici's constituents, the Albuquerque Journal reported "The I's of Texas are no longer on us. 'Chili' is dead. The only time we will use "i" will be when we quote the written word of some Texan".

✻Hearty Beef Chile

2 pounds lean boneless beef
3 tablespoons oil, divided
2 onions, chopped
4 cloves garlic, minced
¼ cup tomato paste
4 fresh or canned jalapeno peppers, stemmed, seeded,
    minced
3 tablespoons chile powder
1 teaspoon salt
1 teaspoon oregano
1 teaspoon cumin
1 teaspoon pepper
2 (15 ounce) cans diced tomatoes with liquid
1 (10 ounce) can condensed beef broth
1 cup water
2 (4 ounce) cans chopped green chiles

- Cut beef into ½-inch cubes. Heat 1 tablespoon oil in kettle and brown cubed beef. Transfer meat to bowl and set aside.

- Heat remaining 2 tablespoons oil in kettle and add onion and garlic. Cook about 3 minutes, stir in tomato paste, jalapenos, chile powder, salt, oregano, cumin and pepper.

- Add tomatoes, meat, beef broth, water and green chiles. Bring to boil and reduce heat. Simmer for 2 hours or until meat is tender and chile thickens. Stir in beans and continue simmering uncovered for about 20 minutes more.

Chile cook-offs in the Southwest usually have three distinct categories: Green, Red and Texas-Style.

Ancho-Spiked Chile

5 ancho chiles
2 cups water
2 tablespoons oil
2 onions, chopped
2 cloves garlic, minced
1 pound lean boneless beef, cubed
1 pound lean boneless pork, cubed
1 fresh or canned jalapeno pepper, seeded, minced
1 teaspoon salt
1 teaspoon dried, crushed oregano
1 teaspoon ground cumin
½ cup dry red wine

- Rinse ancho chiles, remove stems, seeds and veins and place in saucepan with water. Bring to boil, turn off heat and let stand, covered, for 30 minutes or until chiles soften. Pour chiles with liquid into blender and process until smooth.

- Heat oil in large kettle or soup pot and saute onion, garlic and meats until meat is lightly colored. Add jalapeno pepper, salt, oregano, cumin, wine and ancho puree.

- Bring to boil, reduce heat, cover and simmer 2 hours. Uncover and simmer for about 30 minutes or until chile thickens slightly.

Jerry Jeff Walker probably said it best, "If you know beans about chili, you know chili has no beans."

Pecos Pork Stew

2 pounds boneless pork shoulder, cut in 1-inch cubes
2 tablespoon oil
2 onions, chopped
2 bell peppers, chopped
2 cloves garlic, minced
¼ cup fresh chopped cilantro
3 tablespoons chile powder
½ teaspoon dried oregano leaves
1 teaspoon salt
½ teaspoon cayenne pepper
2 (14 ounce) cans chicken broth
2 cups peeled potatoes, cut in 1-inch pieces
1 (16 ounce) package frozen corn
1 (15 ounce) can garbanzo beans, drained

In large roaster, brown meat in hot oil. Stir in onions, bell pepper, garlic, cilantro, chile powder, oregano, salt, cayenne pepper and chicken broth.

Cover and cook on medium heat about 45 minutes or until pork is tender.

Add potatoes, corn and beans. Bring to boil, turn heat down to medium and cook another 30 minutes. Serve with cornbread.

Creamy Chicken Chowder

3 cups cooked, cubed chicken
1 (14 ounce) can chicken broth
2 (10 ounce) cans cream of potato soup
1 large onion, chopped
3 ribs celery, sliced diagonally
1 (16 ounce) package frozen whole kernel corn, thawed
⅔ cup heavy cream or whipping cream

 Combine all ingredients except cream in large soup pot with ¾ cup water.

Cover and cook on low heat for about 45 minutes. Add heavy cream to slow cooker and heat another 15 minutes on low heat. Do not boil.

In 1848 at the end of the Mexican-American War, the peace treaty with Mexico ceded the territories of Nuevo Mexico including what is now Arizona and the territory of California to the United States. In 1912 New Mexico became the 47th state in the Union.

Ham-Vegetable Chowder
Great recipe for leftover ham

1 medium potato
2 (10 ounce) cans cream of celery soup
1 (14 ounce) can chicken broth
3 cups finely diced ham
1 (15 ounce) can whole kernel corn
2 (4 ounce) cans chopped green chiles
2 carrots, sliced
1 onion, coarsely chopped
1 teaspoon dried basil
1 teaspoon seasoned salt
1 teaspoon white pepper
1 (10 ounce) package frozen broccoli florets

💧 Cut potato into 1-inch pieces. Combine all ingredients
   except broccoli florets in large soup pot.

💧 Cover and cook on low heat for 45 minutes. Add broccoli
   to soup pot and cook another 15 to 20 minutes.

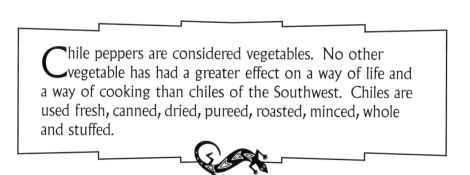

Chile peppers are considered vegetables. No other
vegetable has had a greater effect on a way of life and
a way of cooking than chiles of the Southwest. Chiles are
used fresh, canned, dried, pureed, roasted, minced, whole
and stuffed.

SIDE DISHES

Chile-Corn Queso
A really great dish that's a fun change.

3 eggs
1 (8 ounce) can cream-style corn
1 (15 ounce) can whole kernel corn, drained
½ cup (1 stick) butter
2 tablespoons butter, melted
⅓ cup yellow cornmeal
1 (7 ounce) can green chile salsa
⅛ teaspoon cayenne pepper, optional
1 teaspoon seasoned salt
1 (8 ounce) package shredded Monterey Jack cheese
¾ cup sour cream
1 cup crushed cheese crackers
Cilantro salsa

❀ Preheat oven to 325°.

❀ Combine both cans corn, ½ cup butter, cornmeal, green chile salsa, cayenne pepper, seasoned salt, Jack cheese and sour cream and mix well.

❀ Pour into well greased 10-inch pie plate. Combine remaining melted butter and crushed crackers in small bowl and sprinkle over corn mixture. Bake for 25 minutes. When serving, cut in pie-shaped wedges. Serve with ample spoonful cilantro salsa.

Skyway Super Corn

2 (15 ounce) cans whole kernel corn
2 (15 ounce) cans creamed corn
½ cup (1 stick) butter, melted
1 (8 ounce) carton sour cream
1 egg, beaten
1 (8 ounce) package jalapeno cornbread mix

- Preheat oven to 350°.

- In large bowl, combine all ingredients and mix well. Pour into greased 3-quart casserole dish, cover and bake for 35 to 40 minutes.

TIP: *Make this a one-dish meal by adding 2 to 3 cups cubed, leftover ham.*

Atomic Salsa-Corn

1 (8 ounce) jar hot salsa
1 (16 ounce) package frozen whole kernel corn, thawed
¼ teaspoon garlic powder
½ cup grated Monterey Jack cheese

- Combine hot salsa, corn, garlic powder and ¼ cup water in saucepan. Cook on low to medium heat, stirring occasionally, for 5 to 7 minutes. Pour into serving bowl and sprinkle with cheese.

Fresh Adobe Corn

½ teaspoon chile powder
¼ teaspoon cumin
½ teaspoon salt
1 teaspoon lime juice
¼ cup (½ stick) butter, melted
4 ears fresh corn, husks and silks removed

❦ Moisten chile powder, cumin and salt in lime juice. Add butter and stir until all ingredients blend. Place in small serving bowl.

❦ Place corn in 5-quart pan and cover with cold water. Cover pan, bring to boil and boil for only 1 minute.

❦ Turn heat off, let stand about 2 minutes or until corn is tender and drain. Serve with butter mixture.

Kit Carson Green Chile-Corn Fritters

3 teaspoons baking powder
1½ cups flour
1 teaspoon sugar
½ teaspoon salt
1 egg, beaten
1 (4 ounce) can chopped green chiles, drained
1 (8 ounce) can whole kernel corn, drained
Milk
Oil for frying

❦ Sift dry ingredients in bowl. Add egg, green chiles, corn and enough milk to make batter consistency.

❦ Mix well and drop batter from tablespoon into hot oil and fry until golden brown. Makes about 2 dozen.

Southwest Chayote-Corn

Chayote is very similar to zucchini. Zucchini is used here because it is easy to find.

5 large zucchini, sliced
½ onion, chopped
1 (15 ounce) can cream-style corn
1 (8 ounce) can whole kernel corn, drained
1 (8 ounce) package cream cheese, softened
1 tablespoon flour
1 (4 ounce) can chopped green chiles, drained
1 teaspoon salt
½ teaspoon seasoned pepper
1½ cups cracker crumbs

Preheat oven to 350°.

Cook zucchini and onion in ½ cup water just until tender-crisp and drain well. Add corn, cream cheese and flour, leave on low burner and stir constantly until cream cheese melts.

Add green chiles, salt and seasoned pepper, pour into large casserole and top with cracker crumbs. Bake for about 35 minutes.

The staples of the Indians who roamed Mexico and the New World were chile peppers, beans, corn and squash. From these basic ingredients, regional cuisines in Mexico and America developed into an art form.

Yellow Sunburst Hominy

8 slices bacon
1 onion, chopped
1 tablespoon flour
1 (15 ounce) can Mexican-stewed tomatoes with liquid
1 teaspoon chile powder
½ teaspoon seasoned salt
2 (15 ounce) cans yellow hominy, drained
1 (12 ounce) shredded cheddar cheese, divided

 Preheat oven to 350°.

 Cook bacon in large skillet until it is crisp. Remove bacon and reserve about 2 or 3 tablespoons drippings in skillet. Crumble bacon and set aside.

 Add onion to skillet and cook until tender. In mixing bowl, combine and mix bacon, flour, tomatoes, chile powder, salt and about ¼ cup of liquid in tomatoes and mix well.

 Add hominy and 1 cup cheese. Spoon mixture into greased 2-quart casserole, cover and bake for 25 minutes. Top with remaining cheese and return to oven for about 5 minutes. Before serving, sprinkle with crumbled bacon.

Dried chile peppers must be reconstituted some way to use their flavors and heat in cooking. A whole dried chile may be added to a soup or stew and removed before serving. Chiles may also be ground into a powder and served like salt and pepper or sprinkled into the dish.

Canyonlands Dinner Hominy

2 (15 ounce) cans yellow hominy, drained
1 (7 ounce) can chopped green chiles
¼ cup minced onion
1 (8 ounce) package shredded Mexican 4-cheese blend
1 (8 ounce) carton sour cream
¾ teaspoon seasoned salt
¼ teaspoon pepper

 Preheat oven to 350°.

 Mix all ingredients and pour into medium, greased casserole dish. Cover and bake for 30 to 35 minutes.

Green Beans With Pine Nuts

1 (16 ounce) package frozen green beans, thawed
½ cup water
¼ cup (½ stick) butter
¾ cup pine nuts
½ teaspoon garlic powder
½ teaspoon salt
½ teaspoon black pepper
½ teaspoon celery salt

 Cook beans in water in covered, 3-quart saucepan for 10 to 15 minutes or until beans are tender-crisp and drain.

 Melt butter in skillet over medium heat and add pine nuts. Cook, stirring frequently, until golden. Add pine nuts to green beans and season with garlic powder, salt, black pepper and celery salt.

Chile-Cheese Broccoli-Cauliflower

Anaheim chiles are very similar to New Mexico green chiles. Both are great in this recipe.

1 (16 ounce) package frozen broccoli florets, thawed, steamed but firm
1 (16 ounce) package frozen cauliflower, thawed, steamed but firm
1 (8 ounce) package fresh mushrooms, sliced
½ cup chopped Anaheim chiles
¼ cup (½ stick) butter
¼ cup flour
½ teaspoon salt
2½ cups milk
1 (8 ounce) package shredded Mexican 4-cheese blend

Preheat oven at 325°.

Place steamed broccoli, cauliflower, mushrooms and Anaheim chiles in greased 9 x 13-inch baking dish.

In saucepan, melt butter and add flour, salt and cayenne pepper, heat until well blended. Slowly stir in milk and cheese and cook for 2 minutes, stirring constantly or until mixture thickens.

Pour cheese sauce over vegetables, cover and bake for 30 minutes.

New Mexico green and red chiles are most commonly used in Southwest cooking. Anaheim chiles is one variety of New Mexico chiles and are more readily available in some areas. The two chiles are basically interchangeable in Southwest cooking.

Spinach With Pinon Nuts

1 (16 ounce) package frozen leaf spinach, thawed
¼ cup (½ stick) butter
2 cloves garlic, finely minced
5 green onions with tops, chopped
½ teaspoon seasoning salt
¼ teaspoon celery salt
½ cup pine nuts

Cook spinach according to package directions. Melt butter in saucepan and add garlic, onions, seasoning salt and celery salt. Mix well, pour over spinach and toss.

Place in 2-quart casserole dish and sprinkle pine nuts over top. Place under broiler and brown nuts slightly and serve hot.

Pine nuts are also called pinon nuts and are found inside pine cones. They must be heated to be extracted which is an expensive process. Their rich and unique flavor is further enhanced by toasting them and it increases crispness and texture. They are a special addition to Southwest dishes.

*Spinach Enchiladas

2 (10 ounce) packages chopped spinach, thawed, pressed dry
1 (1 ounce) envelope dry onion soup mix
1 (12 ounce) package shredded cheddar cheese
1 (12 ounce) package shredded Monterey Jack cheese
12 flour tortillas
2 cups heavy cream

 Preheat oven to 350°.

 Make sure all water is pressed out of spinach. Combine
spinach and onion soup mix in medium bowl. Blend in
half the cheddar cheese and Jack cheese with spinach.

 Lay out 12 tortillas and place about 3 heaping tablespoons
spinach mixture down middle of tortilla and roll to close.
Place each filled tortilla, seam side down, into sprayed
9 x 13-inch baking dish.

 Pour cream over enchiladas and sprinkle with remaining
cheeses. Bake, covered, for 20 minutes. Uncover and bake
another 15 minutes. Serves 6 to 8.

Research shows that chiles can boost your metabolism
rate causing your body to burn calories faster.

Southwest Monument Spinach

2 (10 ounce) packages frozen, leaf spinach, thawed
1 small onion, chopped
5 tablespoons butter
3 tablespoons flour
1 (5 ounce) can evaporated milk
1 clove garlic, minced
1 teaspoon celery salt
½ teaspoon black pepper
1 tablespoon worcestershire sauce
1 (4 ounce) can chopped green chiles, drained
1 (8 ounce) package shredded Mexican 4-cheese blend
1 cup buttered breadcrumbs

- Preheat oven to 350°.

- Cook spinach according to package directions. Drain ½ cup liquid from spinach and reserve. Drain remaining liquid from spinach.

- In large skillet sauté onion in butter. Add flour, stir well to remove lumps and pour in milk, stirring constantly. Add ½ cup reserved liquid from spinach and stir constantly until sauce thickens.

- Add spinach, garlic, celery salt, pepper, worcestershire, green chiles and cheese to skillet and stir until cheese melts.

- Pour into prepared 9 x 9-inch baking dish and sprinkle breadcrumbs evenly over top. Bake about 20 to 25 minutes or until dish is thoroughly hot.

Butternut Squash, Corn and Tomatoes

¼ cup (½ stick) butter
1 butternut squash, peeled, seeded, diced
1 onion, finely chopped
1 clove garlic, minced
1 (16 ounce) can diced tomatoes
1 bell pepper, diced
1 (15 ounce) can whole kernel corn, drained
1 jalapeno pepper, finely chopped
½ teaspoon salt
¼ teaspoon black pepper
1 teaspoon instant, dry chicken bouillon

Heat butter in large skillet over medium heat. Add squash, onion and garlic and cook 5 minutes.

Add tomatoes, cut bell pepper, corn, jalapeno, salt, pepper and bouillon to skillet.

Bring to boil, cover, reduce heat and simmer about 5 minutes. Uncover and cook several minutes or until most of liquid evaporates.

Dried chiles such as chipotle, ancho and chile seca may be reconstituted by boiling in water and soaking or steaming them for about 30 minutes to 1 hour.

Baked Squash Casserole

4 to 5 yellow summer squash, sliced
2 to 3 fresh green chiles, seeded, minced
1 onion, chopped
1 tablespoon butter
½ to 1 cup milk
½ teaspoon salt
½ teaspoon garlic salt
¼ teaspoon pepper
1 cup grated cheese

 Preheat oven to 350°.

 In large saucepan boil sliced squash until tender, drain and leave in saucepan.

In skillet saute green chiles and onion in butter until onions are translucent and pour into saucepan with squash. Add milk, salt, garlic salt and pepper and stir.

Pour squash mixture into prepared 8 x 8-inch casserole dish and bake for about 45 minutes or until most of liquid absorbs.

Remove from oven and sprinkle cheese evenly over top, return to oven and cook an additional 5 or 10 minutes until cheese melts.

If dried chipotle peppers are not available, canned chipotles in red adobe sauce or ground chipotle pepper may be substituted.

Sunny Yellow Squash

2 pounds small-medium yellow squash, sliced
2 onions, coarsely chopped
3 ribs celery, diagonally sliced
1 sweet red bell pepper, julienned
1 (8 ounce) package cream cheese, cubed
2 green chiles, seeded, chopped
½ teaspoon sugar
1 teaspoon salt
1 teaspoon white pepper
¼ cup (½ stick) butter, melted
1 (10 ounce) can fiesta nacho-cheese soup
1½ cups seasoned croutons

 Preheat oven to 350°.

 Combine squash, onions, celery and bell pepper in large
saucepan. Add about 1 cup water and cook about 10
minutes or until tender, but still crisp. Drain well.

 While still hot, stir in cream cheese, sugar, salt, white
pepper and butter and stir just enough for cream cheese to
melt and blend. Pour into greased 9 x 13-inch baking dish.
Sprinkle croutons on top and bake for about 20 minutes.

Garbanzo beans or chickpeas originated in Spain and are
served in salads, stews and side dishes.

*Green Chile Calabacitas

Calabacitas translated means little squash and refers to zucchini in the Southwest.

6 cups chopped calabaza or zucchini
5 tablespoons butter
½ onion, chopped
1 bell pepper, chopped
1 (8 ounce) can whole kernel corn, drained
1 (4 ounce) can chopped green chiles
1 (8 ounce) package shredded cheddar cheese
1 teaspoon seasoning salt
1 teaspoon freshly ground pepper
1 teaspoon garlic powder
3 eggs, beaten
1 cup cracker crumbs

 Preheat oven to 375°.

 Steam squash in ⅓ cup water in large saucepan just until barely tender. (Do not overcook.) With butter in skillet, saute onion and bell pepper. Add corn and green chiles and cook on medium heat for 5 minutes.

 Add cheese and seasonings and keep on low heat until cheese melts. Add beaten eggs and squash. Pour into 9 x 13-inch greased baking dish. Sprinkle crumbs over casserole and bake for 30 minutes.

Pecos Squash Mix

1 large spaghetti squash
1 large bell pepper, seeded, chopped
1 large tomato, seeded, chopped
4 to 5 green onions with tops, chopped
3 ribs celery, chopped
½ cup oil
½ cup vinegar
Salt and pepper

Boil spaghetti squash in water for 45 minutes. Remove from water, cut in half and cool. In large bowl combine bell pepper, tomato, green onions and celery.

In separate bowl mix oil, vinegar, salt and pepper and stir well. Pour over bell pepper mixture and stir.

Remove seeds from squash and scoop out flesh with fork. Add to vegetables and stir well. Cover and chill for several hours before serving.

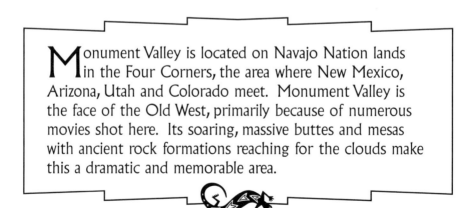

Monument Valley is located on Navajo Nation lands in the Four Corners, the area where New Mexico, Arizona, Utah and Colorado meet. Monument Valley is the face of the Old West, primarily because of numerous movies shot here. Its soaring, massive buttes and mesas with ancient rock formations reaching for the clouds make this a dramatic and memorable area.

Miners' Gold

1½ pounds small yellow squash
1½ pounds zucchini
1 teaspoon seasoned salt
¼ cup (½ stick) butter, melted
½ cup seasoned dry breadcrumbs
½ cup grated cheddar cheese

- Cut both yellow squash and zucchini in small pieces. Place in bottom of slow cooker sprayed with vegetable cooking spray.

- Sprinkle with seasoned salt and pepper. Pour melted butter over squash and sprinkle with breadcrumbs and cheese. Cover and cook on LOW for 5 to 6 hours.

Caramelized Onions
This is very good served with grilled meats.

2 tablespoons (¼ stick) butter
4 to 5 onions, thinly sliced
Salt and black pepper
¼ teaspoon garlic powder, optional

- Melt butter in large, heavy skillet. Add onion slices and cook slowly on low heat. Cook about 30 minutes, stirring occasionally, until onions are soft and dark golden brown.

Stuffed Poblano Rellenos

1¼ cups chopped walnuts
1 cup goat cheese
½ cup ricotta cheese
1 teaspoon cayenne powder
6 large poblano chiles with stems, roasted, peeled, seeded
5 eggs, beaten
¼ cup flour
1¼ cups milk
½ teaspoon salt
½ teaspoon pepper

❦ Combine walnuts, goat cheese, ricotta cheese and cayenne and mix well. Carefully open roasted poblano chiles and stuff cheese mixture into poblanos and close chiles.

❦ Mix eggs, flour, milk, salt and pepper in medium bowl. Dip chiles in egg mixture. Heat oil in deep fryer to 350°. Place chiles in hot oil and fry until golden brown. Remove from oil and drain. Serve immediately.

TIP: For Roasting Chiles: Place poblano chiles over open flame or broil them in oven until outside turns dark brown and blisters on all sides. (Be careful not to burn holes in skin.) Place peppers in plastic bag, seal and allow to sweat for about 15 to 20 minutes so skin will slide off easily. Remove skins and slice through length of pepper on one side. Remove seeds, but leave veins and stem intact.

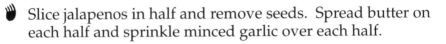
Smoked Jalapenos

10 to 12 jalapenos
3 to 4 cloves garlic, minced
¼ to ½ cup (1 stick) butter
2 tablespoons liquid smoke

Slice jalapenos in half and remove seeds. Spread butter on each half and sprinkle minced garlic over each half.

Place jalapenos in heavy foil. Sprinkle liquid smoke over jalapenos and wrap tightly.

Place foil package over charcoal fire and cook for about 1 hour, if jalapenos are medium to large, less time for smaller jalapenos.

Fried Poblano Rings

3 poblano chile peppers
1 cup flour
Salt and pepper
1 cup milk or buttermilk
Oil

Slice poblanos in rings about ¼-inch wide and remove seeds. Mix flour, salt and pepper in shallow bowl. Dip chile rings into milk and flour mixture.

Carefully place in hot oil in deep-fryer or saucepan with about 3 cups oil. (Oil should be almost to the smoking stage when chiles start cooking.) Fry until golden brown. Lightly salt and serve immediately.

✦Grilled Whole Green Chiles

Serve these delicious chiles whole or sliced in strips called rajas. They add to any Southwest meal.

8 to 10 fresh, whole New Mexico green chiles

 Place chiles on lightly greased grill over low heat. Turn frequently as chiles blister and char on outside, about 2 to 3 minutes. Remove from grill and slide peel away from chiles. Serve whole or cut into narrow strips. Remove seeds to lessen the heat.

Smoke Signal New Mexico Chiles

10 to 12 fresh New Mexico green or red chiles
10 to 12 cloves garlic, minced
1 cup (2 sticks) butter
2 tablespoons liquid smoke

 Slice chiles in half lengthwise and remove seeds. Spread butter on each half and sprinkle minced garlic over each half.

Place chiles in heavy foil. Sprinkle liquid smoke over halves and wrap tightly.

Place foil package over charcoal fire and cook for about 30 minutes to 1 hour.

*Best Pinto Beans

Pinto beans are basic to all Southwest cooking. Good anytime, anywhere.

3 cups dried pinto beans
Water
½ pound salt pork or ham hock
2 to 3 jalapeno peppers, chopped
1 onion, chopped
2 tablespoons chile powder
1 teaspoon garlic powder
1 teaspoon oregano

 Wash beans, cover with water and soak overnight. Drain beans and cover again with water. Add all ingredients and bring to boil. Reduce heat and simmer in covered pot about 3 hours or until beans are tender. (Add water if needed.)

*Frijoles Refritos

Refried beans are just recycled pinto beans and may be used as a side dish, with tacos, burros, on tostadas and in a million other ways.

Leftover, cooked pinto beans
Bacon drippings
Grated cheddar cheese

 Cook leftover beans until most or all of liquid is gone. Drain any excess liquid and mash remaining beans.

 In large, heavy skillet with bacon drippings, fry mashed beans until they are thoroughly heated and mixed with bacon drippings. Serve immediately with cheese on top.

*TIP: **If you want to add more seasonings, try chopped onion, minced garlic, chile powder, cumin and oregano.***

*Frijoles Borrachos

"Drunk beans" make a pretty good dish on any table.

1 (16 ounce) package dry pinto beans
6 cups water
1 (12 ounce) can dark Mexican beer
4 to 6 jalapenos, stemmed, seeded, minced
1 onion, chopped
2 tomatoes, chopped
2 teaspoons worcestershire sauce
Salt

- Sort pinto beans, rinse and soak overnight. When ready to cook, drain beans and pour in water and beer. Bring to boil and simmer for 2 to 3 hours or until beans are almost tender.

- Drain beans, reserving about 2 cups liquid. Pour reserved liquid back into pan and add jalapenos, onion, tomatoes and worcestershire. Taste to adjust seasonings and add salt as needed.

- Simmer 30 to 45 minutes to blend flavors and serve.

TIP: **If you have leftovers, this is great for Refried Beans. See recipe**
on page 159.

One of the best ways to counteract the effects of too much heat from chiles is to rinse the mouth with milk while drinking it. Others believe eating rice or bread may soak up some of the oil from the capsaicin providing all the fire.

Caballeros Trail Beans

2 pounds dried pinto beans
1 medium piece salt pork
5 slices uncooked slab bacon, chopped
2 (10 ounce) cans tomatoes and green chiles
2 to 3 serrano chiles, seeded, minced
1 onion, chopped
¼ teaspoon ground oregano
½ teaspoon ground cumin
2 teaspoons minced garlic
½ teaspoon salt

- Place pinto beans in large saucepan. Rinse and cover with water. Soak overnight or at least 3 hours. Drain and cover with fresh water.

- Add salt pork, bacon, tomatoes, green chiles, serranos and onion. Bring to a boil, add more water if needed, lower heat and simmer for 3 hours or until beans are tender.

- Add oregano, cumin, garlic and salt in the last 30 minutes of cooking.

Lard is traditionally rendered from pork fat and at one time was the only fat available for Southwest cooking. It has a unique, rich flavor that cannot be equaled by vegetable oils or butter. Lard is considered essential for tamales.

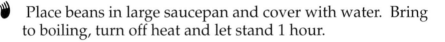
Chile Frijoles

2 cups dry pinto beans
2 onions, finely chopped
2 tablespoons chile powder
1 teaspoon prepared minced garlic
1 (15 ounce) can tomato sauce
1½ pounds lean ground beef, browned
1 tablespoon salt

🌶 Place beans in large saucepan and cover with water. Bring to boiling, turn off heat and let stand 1 hour.

🌶 Drain and add onion, chile powder, garlic, tomato sauce, browned beef and 8 cups water. Cover and cook on medium heat, stirring occasionally, for about 3 hours or until beans are tender. Add salt.

To make pure chile powder, place cleaned, dried chiles on baking pan and bake in oven at 250° until chiles are lightly toasted, but not burned. Remove stems and seeds and grind in food processor. Store in an airtight container.

Arizona Ranch Beans

1 pound dried pinto beans
3 quarts water
½ pound bacon, diced
2 cups cooked, diced ham
1 onion, chopped
2 cloves garlic, minced
2 teaspoons chile powder
½ teaspoon dried oregano
1 teaspoon cumin
2 bay leaves
1 teaspoon salt

Sort beans, place in large saucepan and add enough water to cover beans by 2 inches. Cover and boil for 2 minutes. Remove from heat and soak, covered, for about 1 hour, then drain. Add 3 quarts water and simmer, partially covered, for about 1 hour.

Cook bacon in skillet until crisp. Add bacon and 2 tablespoons of drippings to beans. Add ham, onions, garlic, chile powder, oregano, cumin and bay leaves.

Simmer, partially covered, 2 hours or until beans are very tender. (During cooking, if beans become too dry, add more water.) Remove bay leaves, season with salt and serve hot.

Quick Tamale Casserole

1 (15 ounce) can tamales
1 (15 ounce) can cream-style corn
1 large onion, chopped
1 (12 ounce) package shredded cheddar cheese
1 (4 ounce) can diced green chiles

- Preheat oven to 350°.

- Remove shucks from tamales, slice tamales in 1-inch pieces and place on bottom of prepared 9 x 9-inch casserole dish.

- Sprinkle layers of half the onion, half the cheese, half the green chiles and half the cream-style corn over top of tamales.

- Repeat layers and smooth top layer of cream-style corn. Bake for 30 to 45 minutes and serve.

The most commonly used fresh chiles in Southwest cuisine include the New Mexico green or Anaheim, serrano, jalapeno, poblano and Santa Fe grande. The most commonly used dried chiles include the New Mexico dried red chile, chipotle (dried jalapeno) ancho (dried poblano) and chile seco (dried serrano).

Old Town Bacon Beans

4 slices thick sliced bacon, cooked crisp, crumbled
1 (15 ounce) can kidney beans, drained
1 (15 ounce) can lima beans with liquid
1 (15 ounce) can pinto beans with liquid
1 (15 ounce) can navy beans with liquid
1 (15 ounce) can pork and beans with liquid
1 onion, chopped
2 to 3 jalapenos, seeded, chopped
¾ cup red chile sauce
1 cup packed brown sugar
1 tablespoon worcestershire sauce

 Preheat oven to 350°.

 Combine all ingredients in 3-quart baking dish. Cover and bake for 1 hour.

La Casa Black Beans

3 (15 ounce) cans black beans, rinsed, drained
3 (15 ounce) cans great northern beans, rinsed, drained
1 (16 ounce) jar hot, thick and chunky salsa
½ cup packed brown sugar

 Preheat oven to 350°.

 Combine all beans, salsa and brown sugar in 3-quart baking dish, cover and bake for 1 hour.

TIP: *To change this up slightly, include 1 can pinto beans in the dish and only 2 cans black beans.*

Jalapeno-Cheese Potatoes

5 large potatoes, peeled, sliced, cooked
1 bunch green onions with tops, chopped
1 bell pepper, chopped
2 tablespoons plus ¼ cup (½ stick) butter, divided
1 tablespoon flour
1 teaspoon salt
½ teaspoon white pepper
½ teaspoon garlic powder
1 cup milk
1 (2 ounce) jar chopped pimentos
1 (16 ounce) package cubed, Mexican processed cheese

❧ Preheat oven to 350°.

❧ Place sliced potatoes in greased 9 x 13-inch baking dish.
In medium saucepan, saute onion and bell pepper in
2 tablespoons melted butter and cook until onion is
translucent. Spoon onion and bell pepper over potatoes.

❧ In same skillet melt ¼ cup butter. Add flour, salt, white
pepper and garlic powder. Stir well, add milk gradually
and stir until mixture thickens. Add pimentos and cheese.

❧ Simmer until cheese melts and stir constantly. Pour sauce
over potatoes and bake, covered, for about 25 minutes.

Black beans originated in central Mexico and are rich in
flavor. They are sometimes called frijoles negros.

Roasted New Potatoes

18 to 20 small, new potatoes, unpeeled
½ cup (1 stick) butter, melted
2 (4 ounce) cans diced green chiles
1 tablespoon dried parsley
½ teaspoon garlic powder
1 teaspoon salt
½ teaspoon black pepper
½ teaspoon paprika

Steam potatoes in large saucepan with small amount of water until tender. (Test with fork.) In another saucepan, combine butter, green chiles, parsley, garlic, salt and black pepper. Heat until ingredients mix well.

Place potatoes in serving dish, spoon butter mixture over potatoes and sprinkle with paprika.

Round-Up Potatoes

2 pounds small red new potatoes, sliced
1 bunch green onions with tops, chopped
1 (8 ounce) bottle prepared ranch dressing

In large saucepan, cook potatoes in enough water to cover until tender. Remove from heat, drain thoroughly, add onions and ranch dressing and mix well to coat. Serve warm.

Cheesy Ranch Potatoes

2½ pounds new potatoes, unpeeled, quartered
1 onion, cut into 8 parts
1 (10 ounce) can fiesta nacho-cheese soup
1 (8 ounce) carton sour cream
½ cup milk
1 (1 ounce) package dry ranch salad dressing mix
Chopped fresh parsley, optional

- Place potatoes and onion in large saucepan and partially cover with water. Steam until potatoes are tender and drain.

- In another saucepan, combine soup, sour cream, dressing mix and milk, heat and mix well. Spoon potatoes into serving bowl and pour soup-sour cream mixture over potatoes.

- To serve, sprinkle chopped fresh parsley over potato mixture.

Of the 200 varieties of chiles in the world, 100 varieties are native to Mexico.

Creamy Chile Potatoes

2½ pounds baking potatoes
¼ cup (½ stick) butter
1 large onion, chopped
3 cloves garlic, minced
2 cups milk
4 tablespoons flour
2 teaspoons salt
1 teaspoon pepper
1 (12 ounce) package shredded Monterey Jack cheese
1 (7 ounce) can chopped green chiles
2 cups potato chips, slightly crushed

 Preheat oven to 350°.

 Peel, slice and cook potatoes in large saucepan with just enough water to cover until tender. Prepare 9 x 13-inch baking dish and line bottom with drained potatoes.

 In same saucepan melt butter and saute onion and garlic until onion is translucent. Whisk in flour, remove all lumps, slowly add milk and cook, stirring constantly, until mixture begins to thicken.

 Remove from heat, add salt, pepper, milk, cheese and green chiles and stir carefully. Return to heat, stirring constantly, until cheese melts.

 Pour sauce over potatoes, top with potato chips. Bake for 15 to 20 minutes or until potatoes are thoroughly hot and potato chips are slightly brown.

*Papas Con Chile Verde

2 cups thinly sliced potatoes
½ cup chopped, seeded New Mexico green chiles
1 onion, chopped
1 clove garlic, minced
½ teaspoon salt
2 tablespoons oil
2 to 2½ cups water

- In large skillet brown potatoes, green chiles, onion and salt in hot oil until onions are translucent.

- Pour in 2 cups water and simmer about 20 to 25 minutes. Add water if needed.

Spicy Spanish Rice

1½ cups uncooked white rice
1 (10 ounce) can diced tomatoes and green chiles
1 (15 ounce) can stewed tomatoes
1 (1 ounce) envelope taco seasoning
1 large onion, chopped

- Combine rice, tomatoes, green chiles, stewed tomatoes, taco seasoning, onion and 1½ cups water in large saucepan. Bring to boil, reduce heat and simmer for about 35 minutes or until rice is tender.

TIP: *Make this a main dish by adding 1 pound Polish sausage slices to rice mixture.*

*Spanish Rice

Oil
1 cup uncooked rice
1 small onion, chopped
1 (8 ounce) can tomato sauce
2 cups water
1 teaspoon salt
½ teaspoon pepper
1 teaspoon oregano
½ teaspoon garlic powder
½ teaspoon chile powder

- In large skillet add a little oil, brown rice slowly and brown onion until it is translucent. Stir in tomato sauce and water and bring to boil.

- Reduce heat to simmer, add salt, pepper, oregano, garlic powder and chile powder and stir well. Cover skillet and simmer for about 30 minutes.

"Billy the Kid's Last Ride" is a week-long trial ride that follows the path Billy the Kid took after escaping from the Lincoln, New Mexico jail. The trail ride begins in Lincoln and ends in Fort Sumner where the infamous outlaw is laid to rest.

Brown Rice and Pine Nuts

1 (6 ounce) box instant brown rice
1 (14 ounce) can beef broth
Water
2 ribs celery, sliced
1 small onion, chopped
¼ cup (½ stick) butter
1 teaspoon grated lemon peel
1 tablespoon chopped fresh cilantro leaves
¼ cup toasted pine nuts

❣ Cook brown rice according to package direction, using beef broth plus amount of water called for. Let stand 5 minutes.

❣ Saute celery and onion in butter. Fluff rice and add celery, onion, lemon peel, cilantro and pine nuts.

Fresh cilantro is sometimes called Mexican parsley and is often the secret ingredient that gives Southwest dishes their woodsy, citrus flavor. Coriander is the seed from the cilantro plant and has a much more subtle flavor.

Rice With Avocado

¼ cup (½ stick) butter
1 onion, minced
1 clove garlic, minced
1 cup uncooked rice
½ teaspoon salt
¼ teaspoon crushed oregano
½ teaspoon cumin
1 (14 ounce) can chicken broth
1 (4 ounce) can chopped green chiles
⅓ cup water
2 avocados

Melt butter in medium saucepan, add onion and garlic and cook until tender. Add rice, salt, oregano, cumin, chicken broth, green chiles and water.

Bring to a boil, cover, reduce heat and simmer about 25 to 30 minutes or until rice is tender and all liquid absorbs into rice.

Peel, pit and dice avocados. Fluff up rice with fork, add avocados and toss gently. Let stand 5 minutes before serving.

Anaheim chiles may be substituted for New Mexico chiles if they are not available.

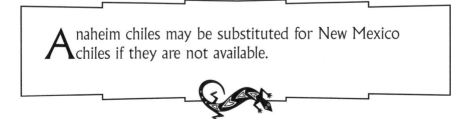

*Arroz Con Queso

1 cup chopped green onion with tops
1 chopped bell pepper, chopped
¼ cup (½ stick) butter
3 cups cooked white rice
1 (8 ounce) carton sour cream
1 teaspoon salt
¾ teaspoon freshly ground pepper
1 (4 ounce) can chopped green chiles
1 (8 ounce) package shredded sharp cheddar cheese
Paprika

 Preheat oven to 350°.

 Saute onion and bell pepper in butter. Remove from heat and combine with remaining ingredients except paprika.

 Toss lightly to mix and pour into greased casserole dish. Cover and bake for 30 to 35 minutes. Garnish with paprika.

Red pepper flakes are made from dried New Mexico red chiles, dried chiles colorado or dried Anaheim chiles. They are ground to large flakes, include seeds and are usually very hot.

Pecos Beans and Rice Supreme

2 (16 ounce) can pinto beans, drained
3 cups cooked white rice
1 (8 ounce) carton sour cream
1 diced bell pepper
2 jalapeno peppers, seeded, diced
1 tablespoon chile powder
1 teaspoon ground cumin
¼ teaspoon ground oregano
½ teaspoon salt
¼ teaspoon black pepper
3 eggs, beaten
2 cups milk
1 (7 ounce) can chopped green chiles, divided
1 (12 ounce) package grated Monterey Jack cheese, divided
1 (12 ounce) package grated sharp cheddar cheese

- Preheat oven to 350°. Grease 3-quart casserole dish.

- Combine beans, rice, sour cream, bell pepper, jalapeno peppers, chile powder, cumin, oregano, salt and pepper. In another bowl, combine eggs and milk.

- Place ⅓ of bean mixture in bottom of casserole dish. Sprinkle with half green chiles and cover with half Monterey Jack cheese.

- Pour 1 cup egg mixture over top. Repeat with another layer of beans, green chiles, Jack cheese and 1 cup egg mixture. Add final layer of beans and pour remaining egg mixture on top.

- Bake for 35 minutes. About 5 minutes before casserole is ready, sprinkle cheddar cheese on top and bake for remaining time.

175

Coronado Chile-Cheese Pie

1 (9 inch) pie crust, baked
1½ cups crumbled guacamole-flavored tortilla chips, divided
1 (15 ounce) can chile beans with liquid
1 (7 ounce) can diced green chiles, drained
3 green onions with tops, chopped
1 (4 ounce) can sliced black olives, drained
1 (8 ounce) carton sour cream
1 (4 ounce) can sliced mushrooms, drained
1 (8 ounce) package shredded Mexican 4-cheese blend

🖐 Preheat oven to 325°.

🖐 In pie crust, line bottom with 1 cup crumbled chips.
Combine beans, green chiles, onions and olives in bowl
and spread evenly over chips. Spoon layer of sour cream
next and sprinkle mushrooms on top. Sprinkle evenly
with cheese.

🖐 Cover dish with foil and bake for about 15 minutes.
Uncover and sprinkle with remaining chips and bake
another 15 minutes. Serve immediately.

100% Chile Powder
Pure, 100% chile powder is made from dried chiles
and is recommended over commercial chili powders.
Commercial chili powder is a mixture of herb seasonings
including dried chiles, oregano, garlic, cumin, cloves and
coriander.

MAIN DISHES

Beef, Chicken,
Pork, Seafood, Game

*Beef Enchiladas

Oil
1½ pounds lean ground beef
1 onion, minced
1 clove garlic, minced
½ teaspoon salt
2 tablespoons chile powder
2 tablespoons flour
1 (15 ounce) can tomato sauce
½ teaspoon salt
½ teaspoon pepper
1 teaspoon cumin
12 corn tortillas
Oil
1 (16 ounce) shredded cheddar cheese, divided

- Preheat oven to 350°.

- Place a little bit of oil in skillet and brown beef, onion and garlic. Add salt and chile powder. Add flour and stir until browned. Stir in tomato sauce, salt, pepper and cumin and simmer 5 minutes.

- Soften tortillas by dipping in a little hot oil and drain. Place about 2 tablespoons meat mixture in each tortillas, top with 2 tablespoons cheese and roll.

- Place seam side down in large baking dish, cover with remaining meat sauce and cheese. Bake for 30 minutes or until hot and bubbly.

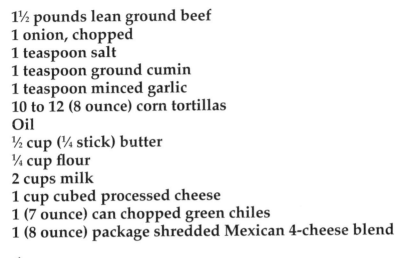

BEEF

*Cheesy Beef Enchiladas

1½ pounds lean ground beef
1 onion, chopped
1 teaspoon salt
1 teaspoon ground cumin
1 teaspoon minced garlic
10 to 12 (8 ounce) corn tortillas
Oil
½ cup (¼ stick) butter
¼ cup flour
2 cups milk
1 cup cubed processed cheese
1 (7 ounce) can chopped green chiles
1 (8 ounce) package shredded Mexican 4-cheese blend

- Preheat oven to 350°.

- In skillet, brown beef and onion. Add salt, cumin and garlic and drain.

- In second skillet, heat a little oil and fry tortillas only enough to soften. Roll equal amount of meat mixture tightly into each softened tortilla until all meat is used.

- Place seam side down in greased 9 x 13-inch baking dish. In first skillet melt butter, add flour and stir to remove all lumps. Slowly pour in milk while stirring constantly. Add cheese and stir until cheese melts. Add green chiles and mix well.

- Pour sauce over enchiladas in baking dish. Top with cheese, cover and bake for about 15 to 20 minutes. Bake for 30 to 35 minutes or until hot and bubbly.

TIP: *Just before cooking, put these enchiladas in the freezer for another day.*

✡Red Chile Enchiladas

This is a Southwest classic.

8 to 10 dried New Mexico red chiles
1 teaspoon oregano
½ teaspoon cumin
1 tablespoon oil
¼ to ½ cup water
12 corn tortillas
Vegetable oil
1 (12 ounce) package shredded cheddar cheese
1 onion, chopped

Put chiles, oregano and cumin in food processor and blend until chiles are in powder form. Strain into heavy skillet, add oil and cook on medium heat until seasonings blend, about 10 to 15 minutes. Add water if needed.

Fry tortillas in hot oil, drain on paper towel and dip both sides in chile sauce. Place tortilla in 1½-quart baking dish, sprinkle cheese and onions and roll up. Place seam side down in dish. Repeat process with all tortillas.

Pour remaining sauce, cheese and onions over top of enchiladas and bake at 350° for about 15 to 20 minutes or until cheese melts. Serve with salsa, refried beans, shredded lettuce or fried egg on the side.

The World's Largest Enchilada is cooked every year in September in Las Cruces, New Mexico. The whole enchilada is 10 feet in diameter.

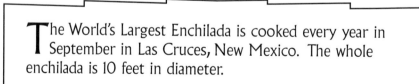

✿Green Enchiladas

1½ pounds lean ground beef
1 onion, chopped
1 teaspoon salt
1 teaspoon ground cumin
1 teaspoon minced garlic
3 cups grated longhorn cheese
1 (10 ounce) can cream of chicken soup
¾ cup evaporated milk
1 (7 ounce) can chopped green chiles, drained
1 (2 ounce) jar chopped pimentos
1 (8 ounce) package shredded cheddar cheese
10 to 12 (8 ounce) corn tortillas
Oil

 Preheat oven to 350°.

 In skillet, brown beef and onion. Add salt, cumin and garlic, then add longhorn cheese. In saucepan, combine soup, milk, green chiles, pimentos and cheddar cheese and heat until cheese melts.

 In second skillet, heat a little oil and fry tortillas only enough to soften. Roll equal amount of meat mixture into each softened tortilla until all meat is used.

 Place seam side down in greased 9 x 13-inch baking dish. Pour cheese-milk sauce over tortillas. Bake for 30 to 35 minutes or until hot and bubbly.

Easy Mexican Fix

6 to 8 hard, round corn tortillas
1 (14 ounce) can beef chile
1 onion, chopped
2 tomatoes, chopped
2 cups chopped lettuce
1 (10 ounce) can cheddar cheese soup
½ cup water
Salsa

🖐 Heat chile in small saucepan and remove from heat. In separate saucepan, heat cheese soup with water until pouring consistency and set aside.

🖐 On large serving platter, lay out round tortillas. Put a little chile on each tortilla and layer onion, tomatoes and lettuce on top.

🖐 Pour hot cheese soup over each mound and top with salsa.

Tortillas are the most popular bread in Mexico and in Southwest cooking. They are hand-made with wheat flour or cornmeal (masa harina) and baked on a griddle.

Gitty-Up Enchilada Casserole

12 corn tortillas
1 pound lean ground beef
1 onion, chopped
1 (8 ounce) can tomato sauce
1 (10 ounce) can enchilada sauce
1 (16 ounce) package shredded cheddar cheese, divided

Preheat oven to 350°.

Tear corn tortillas into pieces and set aside. Brown meat in large skillet and drain. Cook onion until it is translucent.

Remove from heat and stir in tomato sauce, enchilada sauce, half the cheese and tortilla pieces. Pour into prepared casserole dish and bake for 20 to 30 minutes. Sprinkle remaining cheese over top of casserole. Return to oven for 5 minutes.

The Hatch Chile Festival is held every year over Labor Day and celebrates chile growers, chile varieties, chile recipes and a chile-cooking contest. Hatch is the premier area for growing New Mexico chiles.

*Mamacita's Tamale Casserole

1 pound lean ground beef
1 onion, chopped
1 (15 ounce) can Mexican-stewed tomatoes
1 (4 ounce) can chopped black olives, drained
1 (8 ounce) can whole kernel corn, drained
1 (10 ounce) enchilada sauce
1 teaspoon salt
1 teaspoon oregano
½ teaspoon pepper
1 (8 ounce) package cornbread-muffin mix
1 egg, beaten
⅓ cup milk
1 (8 ounce) package shredded cheddar cheese

⚡ Preheat oven to 350°.

⚡ In large skillet, brown ground beef and drain excess fat.
Add onion and cook until onion is translucent.

⚡ Stir in tomatoes, olives, corn, enchilada sauce, salt, oregano
and pepper, cover and cook about 5 minutes. Pour beef
mixture into 9 x 13-inch baking pan.

⚡ In separate bowl, combine cornbread-muffin mix, egg and
milk and pour over top of beef mixture. Bake for 45 to 50
minutes or until cornbread is light brown. Sprinkle with
cheese and serve.

Border Bandit Tamale Dinner

1 onion, chopped
1 tablespoon butter
2 (15 ounce) cans beef tamales
1 (14 ounce) can red chile sauce
1 (4 ounce) can diced green chiles
1 cup grated cheddar cheese
Hot, cooked rice

- In skillet saute onion in butter until onions are translucent. Remove shucks from tamales and place tamales in skillet.

- Add red chile sauce and green chiles, stir and bring to boil. Reduce heat and simmer for about 10 minutes on low. Pour into ovenproof, serving dish and sprinkle grated cheese on top.

- Place ovenproof dish in oven under broiler to melt cheese, remove and serve over hot, cooked rice.

Carlsbad Caverns National Park, in the southeast corner of New Mexico 17 miles from the Texas border, encompasses more than 100 limestone caves with 3 open to the public. An elevator or foot path goes 750 feet below the surface to the Big Room, a 7-acre area with a 200-foot ceiling filled with stalactites, stalagmites and mighty columns.

*Soft Beef Taco Bake

2 pounds lean ground beef
2 tablespoons chile powder
1 tablespoon salt
1 (14 ounce) can kidney beans
1 large onion, chopped, divided
14 to 16 corn tortillas
3 large tomatoes, chopped
1 tablespoon minced cilantro
1 (12 ounce) package shredded cheddar cheese, divided

- Preheat oven to 350°.

- Brown ground beef, add chile powder and salt and cook for about 5 minutes.

- Put several tablespoons of meat, several tablespoons of beans and 1 teaspoon onion in middle of each tortilla, roll up and place side by side in prepared 10 x 14-inch casserole dish.

- Combine tomatoes, remaining onion, and cilantro and sprinkle evenly over rolled tortillas. Spread cheese over top of tomatoes and bake for 10 to 15 minutes or until cheese melts. Serve hot with chips.

TIP: *To make crispy taco shells, spray one side of each tortilla with cooking spray and wrap tortillas in aluminum foil. Bake at 350° for about 10 to 15 minutes to soften tortillas. Remove from oven, fold tortillas in half and put a few in oven-proof dishes with lid. Return to oven and bake until crispy about 15 minutes.*

War Paint Bean-Beef Tacos

1 tablespoon oil
1 onion, finely chopped
1 clove garlic, minced
1 tablespoon chile powder
1 teaspoon cumin
½ teaspoon salt
¼ teaspoon black pepper
½ pound lean ground beef
1 cup canned black beans, rinsed, drained
½ cup canned tomato sauce
6 prepared taco shells
2 cups shredded lettuce
1 (8 ounce) package shredded Monterey Jack cheese
2 tomatoes, diced
4 green onions with tops, chopped

Place oil in skillet over medium heat. Add onions and cook until translucent, but not browned. Add garlic, chile powder, cumin, salt and pepper and cook about 30 seconds.

Stir in beef and cook until browned, about 5 minutes. Stir in black beans and tomato sauce and simmer about 3 minutes.

Fill each taco shell first with beef filling, then lettuce and cheese. Top with tomatoes and green onions.

North of Lincoln National Forest in southeast New Mexico lies the Mescalero Apache Indian Reservation. The Apache people own and operate exclusive recreation facilities that extend from Ruidoso south to Cloudcroft.

*Outlaw Beef Tacos

2 pounds lean ground beef, cooked
2 tablespoons salt
1 (1 ounce) package taco seasoning or fajita seasoning
1 large onion, chopped, divided
3 large tomatoes, chopped
1 (12 ounce) package shredded cheddar cheese, divided
24 corn or flour tortillas, warmed

Season beef with salt and seasoning package. Put 1 to 2 tablespoons of meat, chopped onion, tomatoes and cheese in middle of each tortilla, roll up and serve with salsa and chips.

Tip: Warm tortillas by putting them in microwave or for softer tortillas, put them on slightly damp paper towel and wrap them up before putting in microwave. You don't need a damp paper towel for flour tortillas.

*Burritos

Burritos are flour tortillas filled with any of several ingredients. They may be served any time of day with any kind of filling. Here are just a few suggestions.

Flour tortillas
FILLINGS:

Refried beans	Guacamole	Chiles
Chile con carne	Shredded meatss	Salsa
Chile con queso	Potatoe	
Scrambled eggs	Onions	

Wrap flour tortilla in dry paper towel and cook it in microwave for about 10 seconds. Choose any filling or combination of fillings and put in middle of flour tortilla. Fold 4 sides toward center like an envelope and eat with hands or fork.

*Down-And-Dirty Beef Burritos

1 pound ground beef
1 teaspoon salt
1 tablespoon chile powder
2 onions, chopped
4 to 6 flour tortillas, warmed
1 (15 ounce) can refried beans
1 (8 ounce) package shredded Mexican 4-cheese blend
1 tomato, chopped
Salsa

In heavy skillet brown ground beef with salt and chile powder. Drain grease, add onions and cook until onions are translucent.

In saucepan, heat refried beans. Spread several tablespoons refried beans on warmed, flour tortilla.

Add ground beef, cheese and tomato and roll up like an envelope, folding up 2 ends and rolling. Serve with salsa.

Burritos are traditional Mexican sandwiches made with flour tortillas and a filling. Tortillas are rolled one turn, folded over on both ends to enclose the filling and rolled again tightly. Burritos that are deep fried or baked are called chimichangas.

Empanadas are small pies with meat, vegetable or sweet fillings. They may be deep fried or baked and are served year-round.

✶Adobe Empanadas

DOUGH:
1 (3 and 8 ounce each) cream cheese, softened
½ cup (1 stick) butter, softened
1⅔ cups flour

FILLING:
½ pound lean ground beef
¾ pound ground pork
1 onion, finely chopped
1 teaspoon minced garlic
1 teaspoon ground cumin
½ teaspoon spicy seasoned salt
1 jalapeno, seeded, finely chopped
1 (8 ounce) can tomato puree
¼ cup pine nuts
⅓ cup raisins
1 egg for sealing, beaten

 Preheat oven to 350°.

 In mixing bowl, combine both packages cream cheese, butter and flour; beat until soft dough forms. Wrap in wax paper and chill 1 hour.

 In large skillet, brown ground meats, add onion and saute. Add garlic, cumin, seasoned salt and jalapeno. Stir in tomato puree, pine nuts and raisins and simmer about 10 minutes.

 When dough chills for 1 hour, roll out to ¼-inch thickness and cut with large biscuit cutter. Place spoonful beef-pork mixture on each dough round.

 With finger dipped in beaten egg, spread egg around edges of dough, fold over and press edges with fork. Place empanadas on greased baking sheet and bake for 10 to 12 minutes or until golden grown.

190

✡Chile Verde Con Carne

2 pounds round steak, tenderized
¼ cup (½ stick) butter
6 to 8 New Mexico green chiles, roasted, peeled, seeded
2 small onions, chopped
2 tomatoes, chopped
4 cloves garlic, minced
1 teaspoon salt
½ to 1 cup water, optional

🌶 Brown meat in butter in large skillet. Reduce heat to low and add all remaining ingredients, except water. Simmer covered for about 2 to 3 hours. Stir occasionally and add water if necessary.

🌶 Remove cover, taste for flavor and adjust seasonings as needed.

A uthentic chile has no beans. This simple fact is based on standards adopted by international chile cook-offs in an effort to capture the true flavors of chiles and meats. It is also supported by history and the origins of the dish itself. Texans claim chile originated in their state and cite the "Chili Queens of San Antonio" who sold chile on street corners before the Civil War as well as chuck wagon cooks as probable originators. New Mexicans and Arizonans, however, believe that chile was first made by Indians after the Spanish brought chile peppers to their territories from Mexico City. The best approach for most normal people is never to get in a discussion about chile or chili (the dish) with a Texan, New Mexican or Arizonan.

*Beef-Stuffed Chile Rellenos
These are mild chile peppers stuffed with meat.

1 pound lean ground beef
Oil
1 onion, minced
½ teaspoon black pepper
1 teaspoon salt
2 tablespoons ground coriander
½ teaspoon ground cloves
8 to 10 New Mexico Red chile peppers
1½ cups flour
½ cup cornmeal
1 teaspoon baking powder
Pinch of salt
2 eggs
1 cup milk

● In heavy skillet brown ground beef with a little oil. Add onion and cook until it is translucent.

● Drain excess fat and add ¼ cup water, black pepper, salt, coriander and cloves. Stir well, simmer for about 1 hour or until most of liquid thickens and set aside. Stir occasionally.

● Place chile peppers on baking sheet and place under broiler in oven. Roast peppers until the skins blacken. Remove from oven, turn peppers and roast under broiler until all sides are charred.

● Remove from oven, cool and remove outer skins of peppers. Stuff peppers with meat mixture.

● In medium bowl mix flour, cornmeal, baking powder and pinch of salt. Beat eggs and add to flour mixture. Pour in milk and stir well.

(Continued on next page.)

(Continued)

Wrap stuffed peppers in dough and drop into hot oil of deep fryer. Fry until golden brown, drain and serve immediately with salsa.

*Albondigas
This is a meatball-potato soup.

2 pounds lean ground beef
1 cup breadcrumbs
1 onion, chopped
2 eggs
2 teaspoons cumin
2 cloves garlic, minced
1 teaspoon salt
½ teaspoon pepper
4 tablespoon bacon drippings or butter
2 tablespoon flour
4 cups hot water
3 tablespoons snipped cilantro
½ teaspoon salt
2 large potatoes, cubed

Combine all ingredients, mix well and form into meatballs about 1¼ inches in diameter.

In large skillet heat bacon drippings or butter and sprinkle flour on top. Stir constantly until flour browns. (Do not burn.)

Add hot water, cilantro and salt and continue to stir until liquid boils. Add meatballs and potatoes and simmer until potatoes are done.

193

Meatballs in Chipotle Sauce

1 pound ground beef
1 pound ground pork
3 eggs
1 cup dry breadcrumbs
⅓ cup milk
1 small onion, finely chopped
2 tablespoons snipped fresh cilantro
1 teaspoon salt
1 teaspoon pepper
1 teaspoon dried oregano
Cooked white rice

CHIPOTLE SAUCE:
3 dried chipotle chiles
2 slices bacon, minced
1 onion, minced
1 tablespoon flour
5 tomatoes, finely chopped
2 cups beef broth
¼ cup finely chopped carrot
¼ cup snipped fresh cilantro
½ teaspoon salt
½ teaspoon pepper

Mix meatball ingredients, shape into 2-inch balls and place in large roaster.

Make chipotle sauce by placing chiles in warm water to soak until softened, about 1 hour. Drain and chop finely.

Cook bacon and onion in saucepan. Mix in flour and stir. Add remaining sauce ingredients and simmer 10 minutes.

Pour sauce over meatballs and bring to boil. Reduce heat, cover and simmer 40 minutes. Serve over rice.

Painted Desert Tomato-Cilantro Steak

1 to 1½ pounds well trimmed, tenderized round steak
Salt and pepper
Flour
Oil
2 onions, chopped
5 carrots, sliced
¾ teaspoon garlic powder
1 (15 ounce) can diced tomatoes with liquid
¾ cup salsa
½ cup water
2 teaspoons instant, dry beef bouillon
1 tablespoon dried cilantro
1 teaspoon salt

 Preheat oven to 325°.

 Cut meat into serving-size pieces and sprinkle with salt and pepper. Dredge steak pieces in flour and coat well. Heat oil in large skillet and brown meat on both sides.

 Remove steak to 9 x 13-inch baking dish. Add onions and carrots and cover. In same skillet, combine garlic powder, tomatoes, salsa, water, beef bouillon, cilantro and salt.

 Heat and stir just to boiling point and pour over steak, onions and carrots. Bake, covered, for about 1 hour 10 minutes.

Manana Round Steak With Mushroom-Salsa
Great salsa-gravy with mashed potatoes

1½ pounds lean round steak
1 teaspoon pepper
1 onion, halved, sliced
2 (10 ounce) cans golden mushroom soup
1½ cups hot, thick and chunky salsa

👋 Trim fat from steak and cut into serving-size pieces. Sprinkle with pepper and place in 5 to 6-quart slow cooker sprayed with vegetable cooking spray.

👋 Place onion slices over steak. Combine mushroom soup and salsa and mix well. Spoon over steak and onions. Cover and cook on LOW for 7 to 8 hours.

*Carne Guisada
This is a very easy, very basic Southwest dish that is always a hit.

2 pounds round steak, cubed
Flour
1 tomato, seeded, chopped
1 to 2 jalapenos, seeded, chopped
½ onion
½ green pepper, seeded, sliced
3 small cloves garlic, minced
½ tablespoon chile powder
½ teaspoon cumin
1 (14 ounce) can beef broth

👋 Dredge round steak in flour and brown in large skillet. Add remaining ingredients and simmer about 2 hours until meat is very tender. Add water as needed. Serve over rice.

*Carne Asada or Steak Tampiquena

4 to 6 beef cutlets, tenderized
Salt and pepper
Canola oil
1 onion, chopped
1 (10 ounce) can chopped green chiles
1 (12 ounce) package shredded Monterey Jack cheese

Season cutlets with salt and pepper, brown in skillet about 5 minutes on each side and place on baking sheet. In hot oil saute onion and green chiles. Spoon equal amounts of onion-green chiles mixture on cutlets. Sprinkle cheese on top and bake at 350° until cheese melts.

Ceremonial Green Chile-Stuffed Tenderloin

2 cloves garlic, minced
1 medium onion, chopped
1 tablespoon virgin olive oil
1 (4 ounce) can diced green chiles
½ cup (4 ounces) shredded Mexican 4-cheese blend
½ cup seasoned breadcrumbs
4 (6 ounce) beef tenderloin filets, 2 inches thick

In large skillet, cook garlic and onion in oil until they are translucent. Add green chiles, cheese and breadcrumbs. Stir several times and remove from heat.

Make horizontal slice three-quarters through beef tenderloin. Place green chile mixture between 2 pieces with toothpick to hold mixture in place.

Grill over charcoal or pan fry in large skillet until done.

197

*Classic Fajitas Grande

Traditional fajitas are straight-forward and honest. They don't need a lot of fluff like sour cream, guacamole or fancy ingredients to make them great.

MARINADE:
¾ cup fresh lime juice
½ cup tequila or beer
½ cup virgin olive oil
10 peppercorns
4 cloves garlic, minced
¼ cup snipped cilantro
2 teaspoons ground cumin
1 teaspoon dried oregano leaves, crushed

2½ pounds beef skirt steak
2 green bell peppers, seeded
2 red bell peppers, seeded
2 yellow bell peppers, seeded
2 onions, quartered or sliced
Oil
Flour tortillas, warmed
Pico de gallo or salsa, optional

- Whisk together all ingredients for marinade. Cut skirt steak across the grain into ½-inch wide strips.

- Place meat and marinade in large plastic bag, seal and turn meat several times to coat. Marinate in refrigerator several hours or overnight and turn occasionally.

- Before cooking meat, wrap tortillas in foil and place in oven on low heat to warm. Remove meat from marinade and grill several minutes over hot coals. Before meat is done, move to coolest part of grill and be careful not to overcook. Rub vegetables with a little oil and add peppers and onions to hottest part of grill. Cook until vegetables are tender-crisp.

(Continued on next page.)

(Continued)

Slice onions and cut peppers in strips. Serve meat, peppers and onions with tortillas and pico de gallo or salsa.

TIP: Pico de gallo adds to the fresh, crisp taste of fajitas, but if you don't have time, don't worry about it. Salsa works great and it's more fun to enjoy the meal.

Ranch-House Pot Roast

1 (2 to 2½) pound boneless rump roast
5 medium potatoes, peeled, quartered
2 large green chiles, seeded, chopped
1 (16 ounce) package peeled baby carrots
2 medium onions, quartered
1 (10 ounce) can golden mushroom soup
1 teaspoon chile powder
½ teaspoon dried basil
½ teaspoon seasoned salt

In skillet lightly coated with cooking spray, brown roast on all sides. Place potatoes, chiles, carrots and onions in 4 to 5-quart slow cooker sprayed with cooking spray.

Place browned roast on top of vegetables. In bowl, combine soup, chile powder, basil and seasoned salt and pour over meat and vegetables

Cover and cook on LOW for 9 to 11 hours.

Tip: To serve, transfer roast and vegetables to serving plate. Stir juices remaining in slow cooker and spoon over roast and vegetables.

*Jalapeno-Flank Fajitas

While fajitas are a Texas invention, no doubt native Indians in the Southwest wrapped poor cuts of meat inside tortillas or fry bread with a pepper or two.

MARINADE:
½ cup lime juice
¼ cup tequila
2 tablespoons olive oil
2 cloves garlic, minced
1 fresh jalapeno pepper, minced
1 tablespoon snipped cilantro

2 pounds beef flank steak
1 green bell pepper, seeded
1 red bell pepper, seeded
1 yellow bell pepper, seeded
1 onion
12 flour tortillas

 Combine all marinade ingredients in bowl. Trim fat from meat and place in medium bowl. Pour marinade over beef, cover and chill for about 8 hours. Turn meat several times while in marinade.

 When ready to cook, wrap tortillas in foil and place on side of grill or in oven on low heat to warm. Place meat on grill for about 4 minutes and turn to other side. Add vegetables to grill and cook until grill marks show and vegetables are tender-crisp.

 To serve, cut meat across grain into thin slices about ¼ to ½ inch thick and place on warm platter. Slice peppers and onions and serve with warm tortillas.

TIP: The traditional way to make fajitas is to use skirt steak, but flank steak works just as well.

Desert Chuck Roast

1 (1½ to 2 pound) chuck roast
1 tablespoon chile powder
1½ teaspoons salt
½ teaspoon pepper
½ teaspoon cumin
2 tablespoons oil
2 cups water
4 dried New Mexico red chiles, ground
1 (15 ounce) can Mexican stewed tomatoes
3 carrots, chopped
3 onions, halved
½ green pepper, seeded, diced
2 baking potatoes, chopped

🐾 Preheat oven to 350°.

🐾 Season chuck roast with chile powder, salt, pepper and cumin. In large skillet brown roast on all sides in oil.

🐾 Transfer to large soup pot or roasting pot and pour in water, dried chiles and stewed tomatoes. Cover and cook on low heat for 2 hours. Remove from pot, cool and slice into bite-size pieces. Return roast to pot.

🐾 Add carrots, green pepper and potatoes to pot, cover and cook an additional 1 hour or until vegetables are tender. Add water if needed.

The Fall Chile Festival is held in October in Grants, New Mexico.

*Round-Up Barbecue Beef

1 (4 pound) beef brisket
¼ cup liquid smoke
1 (4 ounce) can diced green chiles
2 cloves garlic, minced
1 tablespoon celery salt
1 teaspoon seasoned salt
1 teaspoon cracked black pepper
¼ cup worcestershire sauce
1 cup prepared hickory barbecue sauce

- Place brisket on foil and coat with liquid smoke, garlic, celery salt, seasoned salt, pepper and worcestershire. Wrap foil tightly and chill overnight.

- Preheat oven to 325°. Bake for 3 hours. Remove from oven, open foil and add barbecue sauce. Do not seal. Turn oven to 300° and bake brisket for 1 hour 30 minutes. Baste occasionally. Slice across the grain.

The capsaicin that produces the heat in chile peppers has proven medical benefits including increasing the blood flow to the lining of the stomach protecting it from ulcers or aiding in the healing of ulcers. In countries with people who eat chile peppers regularly, the percentage of people with cancer is unusually low, suggesting that capsaicin has properties that neutralize some carcinogens.

Kitchen-Smoked Beef Brisket

1 (5 to 6 pound) beef brisket
1 (4-ounce) bottle liquid smoke
1 teaspoon celery salt
1 teaspoon paprika
¼ teaspoon nutmeg
1 teaspoon garlic powder
1 teaspoon onion salt
1 teaspoon seasoned pepper
1 tablespoon brown sugar

❦ Cover brisket with liquid smoke, cover with foil and chill overnight.

❦ Combine celery salt, paprika, nutmeg, garlic powder, onion salt, pepper and brown sugar.

❦ Sprinkle brisket with mixture and cover tightly with foil.

❦ Bake 2 hours at 325°.

❦ Loosen foil and bake 5 hours more at 200°.

❦ Remove meat from pan and set aside at least 1 hour before slicing. Strain any grease from pan juices. Slice brisket very thin across the grain and serve with hot degreased liquid.

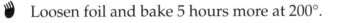

The Gila Wilderness and adjoining Aldo Leopold Wilderness areas comprise the largest, roadless area in the 48 contiguous states. It is in the Gila National Forest located in south central New Mexico and is one of the most important wilderness areas in the U.S.

BEEF

*Beef Flautas
This is great for leftover brisket.

2 to 3 cups shredded beef brisket
1 tablespoon chile powder
1 tablespoon snipped cilantro
2 teaspoons cumin
1 onion, chopped
2 cloves garlic, minced
Canola oil
Corn tortillas

- Season shredded brisket with chile powder, cilantro, cumin and salt and stir. Mix onion and garlic with beef.

- Place several tablespoons shredded brisket in corn tortilla, fold up like envelope and secure with toothpick.

- Heat oil in deep saucepan and carefully drop flauta into oil. Fry until crispy, remove from oil and drain. Serve hot.

Deep-frying is used for many dishes in Southwest cooking. Peanut oil is the most stable oil at high temperatures and has a very high smoke point. Cooking oil should be heated to 350° to 400°. Meats or vegetables should not remain in hot oil for long. The idea is to cook the outside of the meat or vegetable fast to protect the juices and flavors on the inside.

*Chiricahua Chilaquiles

12 corn tortillas
Canola oil
2 onions, chopped
2 cloves garlic, minced
1 bell pepper, seeded, chopped
1 pound lean ground meat
1 (20 ounce) can crushed tomatoes
2 tablespoons chile powder
1 teaspoon salt
1 (12 ounce) package shredded cheddar cheese
1 (5 ounce) can chopped ripe olives, drained

- Cut tortillas into 1-inch squares and fry in hot oil. Add onions, garlic and bell pepper and cook until onions are translucent. Add ground meat and brown. Add tomatoes, chile powder and salt and stir well. Simmer for 30 minutes.

- Pour into 2-quart casserole dish and sprinkle with cheese. Bake at 350° for about 15 minutes or until cheese melts. Top with sliced olives and serve.

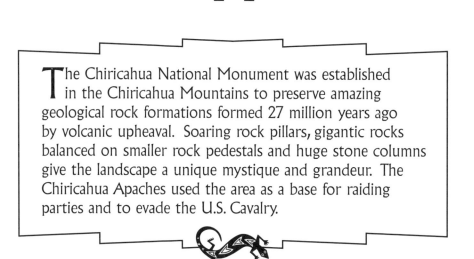

The Chiricahua National Monument was established in the Chiricahua Mountains to preserve amazing geological rock formations formed 27 million years ago by volcanic upheaval. Soaring rock pillars, gigantic rocks balanced on smaller rock pedestals and huge stone columns give the landscape a unique mystique and grandeur. The Chiricahua Apaches used the area as a base for raiding parties and to evade the U.S. Cavalry.

Cilantro-Chicken Cutlets

1½ teaspoons seasoned salt, divided
1 teaspoon seasoned pepper
3 teaspoons snipped cilantro, divided
1¼ teaspoons cumin, divided
6 boneless, skinless chicken breast halves
2 cups breadcrumbs
Oil
3 tablespoons butter
¼ cup flour
2 cups milk
⅓ cup dry white wine
1 (8 ounce) grated Monterey Jack cheese

 Preheat oven to 350°.

 Pound chicken breast halves to ¼-inch thick with mallet or rolling pin. Mix 1 teaspoon seasoned salt, seasoned pepper, 2 teaspoons cilantro and 1 teaspoon cumin. Sprinkle seasonings over chicken cutlets and dip in breadcrumbs.

 Pour oil into large skillet and brown chicken and both sides. Remove to 9 x 13-inch greased baking dish.

 In saucepan, melt butter, blend in flour, ½ teaspoon seasoned salt, 1 teaspoon cilantro and ¼ teaspoon cumin. Add milk, stir constantly and cook until sauce thickens.

 Remove from heat and stir in wine. Pour sauce over chicken and bake, covered, for 45 minutes. Remove from oven, sprinkle cheese on top of each piece of chicken and return to oven for 5 minutes.

Chicken-Chile Roll-ups

8 boneless, skinless chicken breast halves
1 teaspoon salt
½ teaspoon pepper
2 (4 ounce) cans diced green chiles
1 (8 ounce) package shredded cheddar cheese
½ cup (1 stick) butter, melted
2 cups crushed tortilla chips

💧 Layout wax paper on counter, place each chicken breast, flatten to about ¼-inch thickness with rolling pin or mallet and season with salt and pepper.

💧 Place diced green chiles evenly in center of each chicken breast. Sprinkle a little cheese evenly on top of green chiles. Carefully roll up each chicken breasts so no chiles or cheese will seep out and secure with toothpicks.

💧 Place each chicken in small casserole dish and chill several hours or overnight. When ready to bake, roll each chicken breast in melted butter and crushed tortilla chips.

💧 Preheat oven to 350° and bake for about 25 to 30 minutes or until tender.

No other area on earth offers as much high-contrast terrain as the dunes of White Sands and the black lava flows of the Valley of Fires in southern New Mexico. Satellites use this area to calibrate their cameras.

Apache Trail Drum-Sticks

⅔ cup fine, dry breadcrumbs
⅔ cup finely crushed corn chips
1 (1 ounce) package taco seasoning mix
1 (16 ounce) jar taco sauce, divided
2 pounds chicken drum-sticks, skinned

- Preheat oven to 375°.

- Combine breadcrumbs, crushed corn chips and dry taco seasoning mix. Place ½ cup taco sauce in flat bowl. Dip drum-sticks in taco sauce, one at a time, then dredge in crumb mixture. Discard taco sauce used for dipping.

- Place on lightly greased baking sheet and bake for 30 to 35 minutes. Serve with remaining taco sauce.

The Navajo and Apache peoples descended from the Athabascans from Canada and Alaska who traveled south along the Rocky Mountains. The Navajo came to the Southwest sometime around 1200 A.D. and the Apaches came to the area in the late 15th century.

Four-Legged Chicken

4 boneless, skinless chicken breast halves
4 boneless, skinless boneless thighs
4 skinless legs
¾ cup honey
½ cup prepared mustard
½ cup (1 stick) butter, melted
1 teaspoon salt
1 teaspoon curry powder
1 teaspoon minced cilantro

 Preheat oven to 350°.

 In prepared 9 x 13-inch baking dish, arrange all chicken pieces. In bowl, mix honey, mustard, butter, salt, curry powder and cilantro. Spread evenly over all chicken pieces.

 Bake for 30 minutes, remove from oven and baste chicken with pan juices. Return to oven and bake an additional 30 minutes or until chicken is golden brown.

New Mexico is the fifth largest state in the U.S. It is the least populated state of any that border it and it is one of the poorest states.

Home-Style Southwest Chicken

2 cups fine breadcrumbs
1 tablespoon cumin
2 teaspoons chile powder
½ teaspoon salt
½ teaspoon oregano
4 eggs
½ cup prepared green chile salsa
2 cloves garlic, minced
3 to 4 pounds boneless, skinless chicken breast halves
3 tablespoons butter
Iceberg lettuce
Sour cream
1 avocado
1 lime
Green onions with tops, chopped

 Preheat oven to 350°.

 Combine breadcrumbs, cumin, chile powder, salt and oregano in large, shallow bowl and set aside. In separate bowl, beat eggs with salsa and garlic.

 Melt butter in 9 x 13-inch baking dish and melt in oven. Dip chicken pieces into egg bowl and coat with breadcrumb mixture. Place pieces in baking dish and turn each piece in butter. Bake, uncovered, for about 35 to 40 minutes or until chicken is done.

 Place several leaves of iceberg lettuce on plate and serve chicken on top. Garnish with sour cream, avocado slices, lime slices and chopped green onion.

Southwest Chicken-Pot

6 boneless, skinless chicken breast halves
1 teaspoon ground cumin
1 teaspoon chile powder
1 (10 ounce) can cream of chicken soup
1 (10 ounce) can fiesta-nacho cheese soup
1 cup salsa

- In oblong slow cooker sprayed with vegetable cooking spray, place chicken breasts sprinkled with cumin, chile powder and some salt and pepper.

- In saucepan, combine chicken soup, nacho cheese soup and salsa, heat just enough to mix and pour over chicken breasts.

- Cover and cook on LOW for 6 to 7 hours. Serve over hot cooked rice with warmed flour tortillas spread with butter.

Santa Fe Style is known all over the world and has captured the imagination of artisans and artists, actors, singers, jewelry makers, history buffs, architects, cowboys, Indians, adventure seekers, dreamers, developers and designers. In no other city in the Southwest does the culture of the region come together so completely and so richly. More than 13 million people visit Santa Fe annually.

Aztec Creamy Salsa Chicken

6 skinless, boneless skinless chicken breast halves
Oil
1 (1 ounce) package dry taco seasoning mix
1 (16 ounce) jar salsa
1 (8 ounce) carton sour cream

- Preheat oven to 350°.

- Brown chicken breasts in skillet and transfer to greased
  9 x 13-inch casserole dish. Sprinkle taco seasoning
  over chicken and top with salsa. Cover and bake for 35
  minutes.

- Remove chicken to serving plates. Add sour cream to
  juices in pan, stir well and microwave on HIGH for about 2
  minutes. Stir pan juices and sour cream for sauce to serve
  over chicken.

The Grand Canyon in northwestern Arizona records
more than two billion years of the earth's history and is
the best record of earth's formation anywhere in the world.
Fossils found in the layers of earth exposed in the Grand
Canyon tell the story of the development of life beginning
with bacteria and algae.

Chicken Diablo

6 boneless, skinless chicken breast halves
1 (8 ounce) package cream cheese, softened
1 (16 ounce) jar salsa
2 teaspoons cumin
1 bunch fresh green onions with tops, chopped

Preheat oven to 350°.

Pound chicken breasts to flatten. In mixing bowl, beat cream cheese until smooth and add salsa, cumin and onions.

Place heaping spoonful of cream cheese mixture on each chicken breast and roll. (There will be leftover cream cheese mixture.)

Place in greased 7 x 11-inch baking dish. Spoon remaining cream cheese mixture over chicken rolls. Cover and bake 30 minutes, uncover and continue cooking until chicken rolls are light brown.

The Grand Canyon is one of the world's greatest natural wonders. It is more than 5,000 feet deep, 227 miles long and averages 10 miles wide. Grandview Point, elevation 7,400 feet, is thought to be the place where the first Spanish explorers viewed the canyon about 1540.

Red Rock Taco Chicken

3 cups cooked, chopped chicken
1 (1.3 ounce) envelope taco seasoning
1 cup uncooked white rice
½ cup water
2 cups chopped celery
1 red bell pepper, seeded, chopped
2 (15 ounce) cans Mexican-stewed tomatoes
1 (6 ounce) can fried onion rings

 Preheat oven to 325°.

 Combine cooked chicken, taco seasoning, rice, water, celery, bell pepper and tomatoes in greased 9 x 13-inch casserole dish and mix well.

 Cover and bake for 25 minutes, remove cover and sprinkle onion rings over casserole. Return to oven for 15 minutes.

Tip: This is a great recipe for leftover chicken.

The qualities of natural light in the hills of northern New Mexico have made Santa Fe and New Mexico a mecca for artists and artisans. Santa Fe has the second largest art trade in the U.S.

Pollo Delicioso

4 fresh jalapeno chiles, seeded, diced
1 onion, chopped
1 bell pepper, chopped
1 clove garlic, minced
2 tablespoons oil
1 teaspoon ground cumin
½ teaspoon chile powder
1 (10 ounce) can condensed chicken soup
1 (10 ounce) package frozen spinach, thawed
½ teaspoon salt
1 pint sour cream
4 large chicken breasts, cooked, cubed
1 (13 ounce) package corn chips
1 (16 ounce) packages grated Monterey Jack cheese
Paprika

 Preheat oven to 325°.

 In large skillet saute chiles, onion, bell pepper and garlic in oil. Stir in cumin, chile powder and chicken soup.

 Squeeze thawed spinach in paper towels to drain thoroughly. Fold spinach, salt, sour cream and chicken into mixture. Heat, stirring constantly, but do not boil.

 In buttered 9 x 13-inch baking dish, layer ⅓ corn chips, ⅓ cheese and ½ chicken mixture. Repeat layering and top with last layer of corn chips and cheese.

 Bake for 40 minutes or until casserole is hot and bubbly. Garnish with paprika.

Jalapeno Chicken Bark

This one barks a little to get your attention, but it sure is good.

6 boneless, skinless chicken breast halves
¼ cup oil
¼ cup white wine
1 pint sour cream
1 tablespoon flour
1 clove garlic, minced
½ teaspoon salt
¼ teaspoon black pepper
½ teaspoon ground cumin
1 (7 ounce) can whole jalapeno peppers
1 (12 ounce) package Monterey Jack cheese
1 onion, sliced in rounds

 Preheat oven to 325°.

 Brown chicken on both sides in oil. Place in 9 x 13-inch baking dish. In blender, combine wine, sour cream, flour, garlic, salt, pepper, cumin and peppers.

 Blend until smooth to make sauce. Pour sauce over chicken breasts, sprinkle with cheese and top with onion rings. Bake, covered, for 1 hour.

Phoenix is the state capitol and economic center of Arizona. It is also the largest city in the Southwest.

Prairie Spring Chicken

2 pounds chicken thighs
Oil
¾ cup chile sauce
¾ cup packed brown sugar
1 (1.3 ounce) envelope dry onion soup mix
⅛ teaspoon cayenne pepper

❂ Preheat oven to 325°.

❂ Brown chicken pieces in skillet with a little oil and place in greased 9 x 13-inch baking dish. Combine chile sauce, brown sugar, dry soup mix, cayenne pepper and ½ cup water and pour over chicken.

❂ Cover and bake for 20 minutes. Remove cover and bake another 15 minutes to allow chicken to brown. Serve over hot cooked rice.

Taliesin West is home to the Frank Lloyd Wright School of Architecture. Wright, who is generally regarded as America's greatest architect, gained fame in Chicago in the 1890's, but established Taliesin West in 1937. Taliesin is an example of how local materials such as desert rocks and earth can be used to blend architecture with its surroundings.

Easy Green Chile Chicken

6 to 8 boneless, skinless chicken breast halves
Salt and pepper
Flour
Oil
1 onion, chopped
2 ribs celery, chopped
3 tablespoons white wine vinegar
4 tablespoons worcestershire
1 cup white wine
1 (7 ounce) cans chopped green chiles

- Season chicken with salt and pepper. Dredge chicken in flour, brown in hot oil in skillet and remove from heat.

- Combine onion, celery, vinegar, worcestershire, wine and green chiles and mix well. Pour marinade over chicken in skillet, cover and cook about 30 to 45 minutes. Uncover and cook or until chicken juices are clear and chicken breasts are slightly brown. Serve over rice.

The Four Corners area is the only place in the U.S. where four states join. It is possible to stand with one foot in New Mexico, one foot in Arizona, one arm in Colorado and the other arm in Utah.

South-of-the-Border Chicken

8 skinless, boneless chicken breasts
1 (8 ounce) package shredded Monterey Jack cheese
½ cup grated cheddar cheese
1 (4 ounce) can chopped green chiles
1 teaspoon cilantro
3 tablespoon dehydrated onions
⅓ cup butter
2 teaspoons cumin
1 teaspoon chile powder
1½ cups crushed tortilla chips

- Preheat oven to 350°.

- Pound chicken breasts flat. In bowl, mix cheeses, chiles, cilantro and onions. Place 2 to 3 tablespoons cheese mixture on each chicken breast, roll each and place seam side down in greased casserole dish.

- In saucepan melt butter and add cumin and chile powder. Pour over chicken.

- Bake covered for 35 minutes. About 15 minutes before chicken is done, uncover and top with crushed chips. Return to oven and bake 5 more minutes.

Arizona and New Mexico became states in 1912. They are the fourth and fifth largest states, but are two of the least populated states in the U.S. Phoenix, Tucson, Santa Fe, Albuquerque and Las Cruces account for about 60% of the total population of the two states.

*Mole Con Pollo Y Arroz

Mole is a traditional Mexican sauce that is well known all over the world. Chocolate is the secret ingredient used to make the sauce rich, but not overly sweet.

1 cup chopped onion
2 cloves garlic, chopped
1 (8 ounce) package slivered almonds
¼ teaspoon black pepper
1 (1 ounce) square bittersweet chocolate
1 (15 ounce) can tomato sauce
2 (7 ounce) cans green chile salsa
2 cups cooked, chopped chicken
1 cup rice, cooked
Avocado
Lime
Sour cream

- Heat a little oil in skillet and cook onion, garlic and almonds until onions are translucent. Add pepper and chocolate and heat on low until chocolate melts. Stir constantly.

- Pour tomato sauce, green chile salsa and chocolate mixture into blender and process until smooth. Pour sauce in skillet and add chicken. Stir to mix well and simmer for about 5 to 10 minutes.

- Serve over hot rice and garnish with avocado and lime slices and a dollop of sour cream.

Mole is a smooth, rich, dark red sauce usually containing a blend of garlic, onion and various chiles and seeds, such as pumpkin seeds called pepitas. A small amount of chocolate makes the sauce a richer flavor and color without adding a sweet flavor.

Pow Wow Chicken

3 onions, chopped
3 bell peppers, chopped
1 teaspoon garlic powder
Oil
2 (10 ounce) cans chopped tomatoes and green chiles
1 (16 ounce) package cubed processed cheese
1 (16 ounce) package shredded cheddar cheese
6 cups cooked, chopped chicken
1 pint sour cream
1 (4 ounce) jar pimentos
Cooked rice
Tortilla chips, crushed

Cook onion, bell peppers and garlic in a little oil. Add tomatoes and green chiles and bring to boil. Reduce heat and simmer about 15 to 20 minutes or until slightly thick.

Add cheeses and heat slowly until cheese melts. Add chicken, sour cream and pimentos. Heat until hot, but do not boil.

To serve, place rice on plate and top with crushed chips. Spoon chicken-cheese mixture over rice and chips. Serve immediately.

New Mexico is known as the Sunshine State because the sun shines 70% of the time. Its nickname is the Land of Enchantment because of the vibrant colors and hues seen in the mountains, sky and mesas.

*Slow-Cook Arroz Con Pollo

This is a classic Southwest chicken and rice dinner, but cooked
conveniently in a slow cooker.

3 to 4 pounds boneless, skinless chicken breasts and thighs
1 (15 ounce) can Mexican-stewed tomatoes
1½ cups uncooked long-grain rice
1 (0.28 ounce) package yellow rice seasoning mix
2 (14 ounce) can chicken broth
1 clove garlic, minced
1 teaspoon oregano
1 teaspoon chile powder
1 teaspoon black pepper

In large slow cooker sprayed with vegetable cooking spray, combine all ingredients plus ¾ cup water and stir well. Cover and cook on LOW for 7 to 8 hours or on HIGH for 3½ to 4 hours.

Bacon-Wrapped Fiesta Chicken

1 (2.5 ounce) jar dried, sliced beef
6 boneless, skinless chicken breast halves
6 slices bacon
1 (10 ounce) can fiesta nacho soup
1 (10 ounce) can golden mushroom soup
1 (6.2 ounce) package parmesan-butter rice, cooked

Place slices of dried beef in bottom of 5-quart slow cooker. Roll each chicken breast half in slice of bacon. Place over dried beef.

Spoon fiesta nacho soup and mushroom soup and ⅓ cup water over chicken. Cover and cook on LOW for 7 to 8 hours. Serve over hot cooked rice.

Tortilla Flats Chicken Bake

6 (6-inch) corn tortillas
3 cups leftover chicken, cubed
1 (10 ounce) package frozen whole kernel corn
1 (15 ounce) can pinto beans with liquid
1 (16 ounce) hot jar salsa
¼ cup sour cream
1 tablespoon flour
3 tablespoons snipped fresh cilantro
1 (8 ounce) package shredded 4-cheese blend

Cut tortillas into 6 wedges. In bottom of slow cooker sprayed with vegetable cooking spray, place half wedges of tortillas.

Place remaining wedges on cooking sheet, bake about 10 minutes at 350° and set aside. Layer chicken, corn and beans over tortillas in slow cooker.

In bowl combine salsa, sour cream, flour and cilantro and pour over corn and beans. Cover and cook on LOW for 3 to 4 hours. When ready to serve, place baked tortillas wedges on top of each serving.

Warming Tortillas
Tortillas may be warmed in any of the following ways.
- Brushed with oil or butter and placed on hot grill.
- Placed on hot griddle or skillet and turned.
- Wrapped in aluminum foil and baked at 300° until hot.
- Wrapped in slightly damp paper towel and microwaved on HIGH for about 45 seconds for 5 tortillas.

Spicy Chicken-Enchilada Casserole

1 onion, chopped
2 tablespoons oil
1 (15 ounce) can stewed tomatoes with liquid
1 (8 ounce) can tomato sauce
1 (4 ounce) can chopped green chiles
1 (1 ounce) package enchilada sauce mix
1 clove garlic, minced
½ teaspoon salt
3 to 4 cups cooked, shredded chicken
12 corn tortillas
2 (2 ounce) cans sliced black olives
1 (16 ounce) package grated Monterey Jack cheese

🐾 Preheat oven to 350°.

🐾 In large roaster or kettle, saute onion in oil until translucent, but not brown. Add tomatoes, tomato sauce, green chiles, enchilada sauce mix, garlic, salt and chicken. Bring to boil, turn heat down and simmer 15 minutes.

🐾 In greased 9 x 13-inch baking pan, place 4 tortillas and spread evenly with ⅓ chicken mixture over top. Add ⅓ olives and cheese and spread evenly. Repeat layers twice, but reserve final layer of cheese.

🐾 Cover and bake for 35 minutes. Remove cover from casserole and sprinkle remaining cheese over top. Return to oven for 5 minutes.

Pimento-Chicken Enchilada Bake

12 corn tortillas
1 (10 ounce) can cream of mushroom soup
1 (10 ounce) can cream of chicken soup
1 cup milk
1 small onion, chopped
2 (4 ounce) cans diced, green chiles
2 (4 ounce) jars diced pimentos, drained
5 boneless, skinless chicken breast halves, cooked
1 (16 ounce) package shredded cheddar cheese

 Preheat oven to 350°.

 Cut tortillas into 1-inch strips and lay half of them in bottom of prepared casserole dish. Mix mushroom soup, chicken soup, milk, onion, green chiles and pimentos in saucepan and heat just enough to mix.

 Chop cooked chicken and place half on top of tortilla strips in greased casserole dish. Pour half of sauce on top of chicken, repeat tortilla layer and sauce layer.

 Cover and bake for 45 minutes. Sprinkle cheese over casserole, return to oven and bake another 5 minutes.

TIP: If you want to make this dish in advance, top with cheese and chill overnight. Bake the next day when you need it.

*Green Chile-Chicken Enchilada Casserole

This classic casserole is good for all occasions. If you don't want to cook a whole chicken, use 6 to 8 boneless, skinless chicken breasts halves. It will save you some time.

1 whole chicken
1 large onion, chopped
3 ribs celery, chopped
1 tablespoon butter
Salt and pepper
1 (7 ounce) can chopped green chiles
1 cup milk
1 (10 ounce) can cream of chicken soup
1 (10 ounce) can cream of mushroom soup
10 corn tortillas, cut into strips
1 (12 ounce) package shredded cheddar cheese

 Preheat oven to 350°.

 Bake chicken in covered baking pan with 1½ cups water, onion, celery, butter, salt and pepper for 1 hour or until juices run clear.

 Remove from oven, remove chicken to platter to cool and reserve 1 cup chicken stock. When chicken cools, remove meat from bone.

 Combine green chiles, milk, reserved chicken stock, cream of chicken soup and cream of mushroom soup in saucepan and heat just enough to mix.

 In prepared, 9 x 13-inch casserole dish, place half of tortillas in bottom of dish, cover with half chicken and half soup mixture and repeat layers.

 Cover and bake for about 30 minutes. Sprinkle cheese on top of casserole and bake another 5 minutes.

*Easy Chicken Enchiladas

12 corn tortillas
1 (10 ounce) can golden mushroom soup
1 (10 ounce) can cream of chicken soup
1 cup milk
1 small onion, chopped
2 (7 ounce) cans green chile salsa
4 to 5 boneless, skinless chicken breast halves, cooked
1 (16 ounce) package shredded cheddar cheese

🌶 Cut tortillas into 1-inch strips and lay half of them in bottom of prepared casserole dish. Mix mushroom soup, cream of chicken soup, milk, onion and salsa in saucepan and heat just enough to mix.

🌶 Chop cooked chicken and place half on top of tortilla strips in casserole. Pour half of sauce on top of chicken, repeat tortilla layer and sauce layer. Top with cheese and chill overnight.

🌶 Preheat oven to 350° and bake 1 hour or until enchiladas are slightly firm. Serve hot.

Carson National Forest is home to the 13,161-foot Wheeler Peak, the highest point in New Mexico. The U.S. Congress designated a portion of the Rio Chama running through Carson National Forest as a National Wild and Scenic River.

*Stampede Chicken Enchiladas

This classic enchilada dish will make your herd excited. Get ready for the stampede.

2 cups cooked, shredded chicken
1 (4 ounce) can chopped green chiles
1 (7 ounce) can green chile salsa
1 onion, minced
6 chicken bouillon cubes
½ teaspoon salt
2½ cups whipping cream
Oil
12 corn tortillas
1 (16 ounce) package shredded Monterey Jack cheese
1 (8 ounce) carton sour cream

 Preheat oven to 350°.

 Combine chicken, green chiles, green chile salsa and onion. Place bouillon cubes, salt and cream in saucepan and heat until bouillon dissolves, but do not boil.

 Heat oil in skillet and dip each tortilla into oil for about 5 seconds to soften. Drain on paper towels. Dip each tortilla into saucepan with cream and coat each side. Fill each tortilla with chicken mixture.

 Roll and place seam side down in baking dish. Pour remaining cream over enchiladas and sprinkle with cheese. Bake uncovered for 30 to 35 minutes. When ready to serve, top with dollops of sour cream.

*Tomatillo-Chicken Enchiladas

2 (13 ounce) cans tomatillos, drained
1 (7 ounce) can chopped green chiles
2 tablespoons oil
1 onion, chopped
1 clove garlic, minced
1 (14 ounce) can chicken broth
¼ cup oil
12 corn tortillas
3 cups shredded, cooked chicken
1 (12 ounce) packages shredded Monterey Jack cheese
1 (8 ounce) carton sour cream

🔥 Preheat oven to 350°.

🔥 Combine tomatillos and green chiles in blender and
process. In large skillet, heat 2 tablespoons oil, add onion
and garlic and cook until onion is translucent. Stir in puree
and chicken broth. Simmer uncovered until sauce reduces
to consistency of canned tomato sauce.

🔥 In another skillet, heat ¼ cup oil and cook tortillas about 3
seconds on each side. Dip softened tortilla into tomatillo
mixture. Lay sauced tortilla on plate. Place ¼ cup chicken
and 2 tablespoons cheese across tortilla and roll to close.

🔥 Place enchilada, seam side down in 15 x 10-inch baking
pan. Repeat until all tortillas are filled. Spoon remaining
sauce over enchiladas and reserve remaining cheese.

🔥 Cover and bake for about 30 minutes. Uncover and
top with reserved cheese. Bake another 10 minutes,
uncovered. When ready to serve, top each enchilada with
spoonful sour cream.

Quick-Draw Taco Chicken

6 to 8 boneless, skinless chicken breast halves
4 tablespoons (½ stick) butter
1 (8 ounce) can taco sauce
2 (4 ounce) cans chopped green chiles
1 clove garlic, minced

🖐 Place chicken in large skillet and brown on all sides in butter. Add taco sauce, green chiles and garlic and stir well.

🖐 Cover skillet and cook on low to medium about 15 to 20 minutes or until chicken juices are clear. Serve over rice.

TIP: If you are tired of boneless, skinless chicken breasts, substitute legs and thighs.

*Easy Crispy Chicken Tacos

Everybody goes for this classic. Crispy taco shells with chicken, beef or fish make great Southwest treats.

4 to 6 boneless, skinless chicken breast halves, cooked, chopped
8 to 10 taco shells, warmed
1 cup diced tomato, drained
½ cup diced onion
1 cup chopped lettuce
1 (12 ounce) package shredded cheddar cheese
1 (8 ounce) jar spicy salsa

🖐 Make tacos by filling each taco shell with chicken, tomato, onion, lettuce and cheese. Serve with salsa.

*Soft Chicken-Taco Bake

6 boneless, skinless chicken breast halves
1 (1 ounce) package taco seasoning
1 tablespoon salt
1 (15 ounce) can kidney beans, rinsed, drained
1 large onion, chopped, divided
12 corn tortillas
1 cup half-and-half cream
3 large tomatoes, chopped
1 tablespoon minced cilantro
1 (12 ounce) package shredded cheddar cheese, divided

Preheat oven to 325°.

Boil chicken in just enough water to cover. When chicken is cooked and tender, season with taco seasoning and salt. Cool and chop or shred chicken.

Place several tablespoons of meat, several tablespoons of beans and 1 teaspoon onion in middle of each tortilla, roll up and place side by side in prepared 9 x 13-inch casserole dish. Pour cream over rolled tortillas.

Combine tomatoes, remaining onion and cilantro and sprinkle evenly over rolled tortillas. Spread cheese over top of tomatoes and bake uncovered for 20 minutes or until cheese melts. Serve hot with Spanish rice.

To make pure chile powder, clean chiles and remove stems and seeds. Grind in food processor and store in airtight container.

*Flautas de Pollo

Traditional flautas are filled with beef, chicken or pork and work as a main course, appetizer or side dish.

1 cup cooked, minced chicken
12 flour tortillas
Oil
Guacamole
Salsa

❯ Spoon 1 rounded tablespoon chicken on center of each tortilla and roll into tight tube. Heat about 1 inch of oil to about 350° in 4-quart roaster or Dutch oven.

❯ Fry flautas in oil, turn once to brown on both sides and drain. Serve with choice of guacamole or salsa.

*Chimichangas Con Pollo

Chimichangas are stuffed tortillas that are deep-fried. They are really deep-fried burritos. Tucson claims to be the birthplace of the chimichanga or chimi.

4 to 6 boneless, skinless chicken breast halves, cooked,
**   shredded**
3 to 4 New Mexico green chiles, roasted, peeled, chopped
2 tomatoes, peeled, seeded, chopped
1 onion, chopped finely
6 to 8 flour tortillas
1 (8 ounce) package shredded Mexican 4-cheese blend
Red or green chile sauce

❯ Combine chicken, green chiles, tomatoes and onion and stir well to mix. Divide mixture evenly onto tortillas and top with cheese. Fold ends like envelope, roll and secure with toothpick.

❯ Place in deep fryer with oil heated to 350° and fry until golden brown. Drain and serve with chile sauce.

White Lightning Chile

1½ cups dried navy beans
3 (14 ounce) cans chicken broth
2 tablespoons (¼ stick) butter
1 cup water
1 onion, chopped
1 clove garlic, minced
3 cups chopped, cooked chicken
1 (4 ounce) can chopped green chiles
½ teaspoon sweet basil
½ teaspoon white pepper
1½ teaspoons ground cumin
½ teaspoon dried oregano
⅛ teaspoon cayenne pepper
⅛ teaspoon ground cloves
6 (8 inch) flour tortillas
Grated Monterey Jack cheese
Salsa

Wash beans and place in Dutch oven. Cover with water 2 inches above beans and soak overnight. Drain beans, add broth, butter, water, onion and garlic and bring to boil. Reduce heat, cover and simmer 2 hours 30 minutes, stirring occasionally.

With potato masher, mash half of beans several times. Add chicken, green chiles, basil, white pepper, cumin, oregano, cayenne pepper and cloves. Bring to boil, reduce heat, cover and simmer another 30 minutes.

With kitchen shears, make 4 cuts in each tortilla toward center, but not through center. Line serving bowls with tortillas, overlapping cut edges. Spoon in chile and top with cheese or salsa.

Lime-Salsa Campsite Chicken

MARINADE:
¼ cup oil
1 (10 ounce) jar green chile salsa
1½ tablespoons lime juice
½ teaspoon sugar
1 teaspoon garlic powder
1 teaspoon ground cumin
½ teaspoon ground oregano

6 boneless, skinless chicken breast halves

Combine all marinade ingredients and mix well. Add chicken breasts and marinate for 3 to 4 hours.

Cook over hot coals for about 10 to 15 minutes, turning occasionally and basting with remaining marinade.

Arizonans take Southwest cooking beyond chiles and give it a tropical, western touch that adds to Mexican spices. Fresh fruit salsas, unique meat and fruit combinations and mesquite grilling are all favorites in this part of the Southwest. Beef steaks, Mexican food, chimichangas and prickly pear margaritas may be found anywhere in the state and are always special treats.

✡Grilled Chicken Fajitas

6 skinless, boneless chicken breast halves
¼ cup sesame seeds
Cayenne pepper
Seasoned salt
1 red or green bell pepper
1 onion
12 flour tortillas, warmed

🌶 Pound chicken breasts between pieces of wax paper. Sprinkle both sides of chicken breasts with sesame seeds, cayenne pepper and seasoned salt. Slice bell pepper into strips and slice onion twice to make 3 thick slices.

🌶 Grill chicken breasts, bell pepper and onion over charcoal fire. Cook about 5 minutes on each side. Cut chicken breasts into thin strips.

🌶 To assemble, place several strips chicken, bell pepper and onion in center of tortilla. Top with some avocado, salsa or sour cream. Fold over and serve.

TIP: Traditional fajitas do not include sour cream, guacamole or chopped avocado, but you don't have to be traditional.

The prickly pear cacti flourish in the deserts of the Southwest. Nopales are the oval-shaped pads or leaves of the nopal or prickly pear. They have a delicate, slightly tart flavor and are available year-round in Mexican markets. A vegetable peeler can remove the thorns and the flesh is cut into strips, simmered in water and served on scrambled eggs, salads, salsas and meats. Nopalitos are diced nopales and are pickled or canned in water.

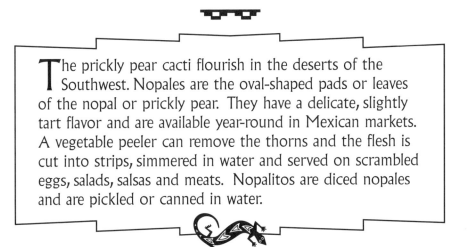

*Tamale-Stuffed Turkey

This classic stuffed turkey is served for holidays and special occasions and is quite a feast.

1 (12 to 16 pound) turkey
1 (9 x 9 inch) pan cornbread

 Allow 3 to 4 days to thaw turkey in refrigerator. When possible remove neck, liver and gizzard to thaw. Prepare cornbread 1 day before making stuffing.

SAUCE:
2 (10 ounce) cans enchilada sauce
3 cups water
2 (10 ounce) cans chicken broth
2 cloves garlic, minced
1 tablespoon chile powder
1 teaspoon salt
1 teaspoon poultry seasoning
1 onion, chopped

 In saucepan combine enchilada sauce, water, chicken broth, garlic, chile powder, salt, poultry seasoning and onion and simmer for 3 to 4 hours. (Add more water or chicken broth if necessary.)

STUFFING:
24 tamales, chopped
1 (8 ounce) package hot sausage
2 onions, quartered
2 ribs celery, chopped
3 tablespoons butter
1 (10 ounce) can chicken broth
2 eggs, beaten
1 teaspoon cumin
½ teaspoon salt
½ teaspoon pepper

(Continued on next page.)

(Continued)

 Crumble cornbread in large bowl, add chopped tamales and set aside. Cook sausage in large skillet, drain and set aside.

 Saute onions and celery in butter until translucent and add to sausage. Pour chicken broth, eggs, cumin, salt and pepper into cornbread mixture. Add sausage and mix gently. Preheat oven to 425°.

 Stuff mixture into cavity of turkey gently and close skin over opening. (Bind if necessary.) Rub entire turkey with butter and lightly salt and pepper.

 Place turkey in roasting pan, breast side up. Pour sauce over turkey, put lid on or cover loosely with foil. Baste occasionally with sauce in pan.

 Reduce oven temperature to 325° and cook for about 4 hours. Remove lid to brown and cook another 30 minutes or until juices run clear. (Do not overcook or let turkey dry out. Continue to baste.)

TIP: The turkey is done when meat thermometer in thigh registers 180° to 185° and leg joint moves freely.

ANOTHER TIP: Jiffy makes a great cornbread mix that is easy and fast.

Slow-Cook Chicken Fajitas

This is a convenient way to have a popular one-pot dinner.

2 pounds boneless, skinless chicken breast halves
1 onion, thinly sliced
1 sweet red bell pepper, julienne
1 teaspoon ground cumin
1½ teaspoons chile powder
1 tablespoon lime juice
½ cup chicken broth
8 to 10 warmed flour tortillas
Guacamole
Sour cream
Tomatoes

- Cut chicken into diagonal strips and place in slow cooker sprayed with vegetable cooking spray.

- Top with onion and bell pepper. In bowl, combine cumin, chile powder, lime juice and chicken broth and pour over chicken and vegetables. Cover and cook on LOW for 5 to 7 hours.

- When serving, spoon several slices of chicken mixture with sauce into center of each warm tortilla and fold. Serve with guacamole, sour cream, lettuce or tomatoes.

Creamy Turkey Enchiladas

2 tablespoons butter
1 onion, finely chopped
3 green onions with tops, chopped
½ teaspoon garlic powder
½ teaspoon seasoned salt
1 (7 ounce) can chopped green chiles
2 (8 ounce) packages cream cheese, softened
3 cups diced turkey or chicken
8 (8 inch) flour tortillas
2 (8 ounce) cartons whipping cream
1 (16 ounce) package shredded Monterey Jack cheese

🦃 Preheat oven to 325°.

🦃 Add butter to large skillet and saute onions until translucent. Add garlic powder, seasoned salt and green chiles. Stir in cream cheese. Heat and stir until cream cheese melts. Add diced chicken.

🦃 Lay out 8 tortillas and spoon about 3 heaping tablespoons turkey mixture on each tortilla. Roll up tortillas and place seam side down in lightly greased 9 x 13-inch baking dish.

🦃 Pour whipping cream over enchiladas and sprinkle cheese on top. Bake uncovered for 20 minutes.

Franciscan Tortilla-Sausage Bake

1½ pounds bulk pork sausage
1 (16 ounce) carton small-curd cottage cheese
2 tablespoons flour
1 (24 ounce) jar prepared spaghetti sauce
2 cloves garlic, minced
1 teaspoon basil
1 teaspoon oregano
10 flour tortillas
1 (12 ounce) package grated mozzarella cheese

🐾 Preheat oven to 350°.

🐾 In large skillet brown sausage and cook until all pink is gone. Drain excess fat. Add cottage cheese and flour to mixture, mix well and cook about 5 minutes.

🐾 In separate bowl, pour in spaghetti sauce, garlic, basil and oregano and mix well. Pour about half of spaghetti sauce into meat mixture, mix well and set remaining sauce aside.

🐾 Lay flour tortillas flat and spoon 10 equal servings of meat-sauce in each tortilla. Roll up and place side by side, seam side down in prepared 9 x 13-inch baking dish. Pour remaining spaghetti sauce over top of rolled tortillas.

🐾 Cover and bake for about 35 to 40 minutes. Remove from oven, uncover and sprinkle mozzarella cheese on top. Return to oven and bake another 5 minutes or until cheese melts.

Spaghetti New Mexico-Style

1 pound mild bulk pork sausage
1 large onion, chopped
2 cloves garlic, minced
2 tablespoons seeded, chopped, pickled jalapenos
1 cup dry white wine
1 (24 ounce) jar prepared spaghetti sauce
1 (1 pound) package spaghetti
Fresh grated parmesan cheese

- In large skillet brown pork sausage and cook on medium until all pink is gone. Stir to break up large pieces. Drain excess fat.

- Add onion, garlic and jalapeno peppers and cook until onion is translucent. Pour in wine and stir well. Add spaghetti sauce and mix well. Simmer for 10 to 15 minutes with skillet covered.

- Cook spaghetti according to package directions and drain. Serve individual portions of spaghetti and pour sauce on top or mix spaghetti and sauce before serving. Serve with fresh grated parmesan cheese.

The Navajo Nation Fair is the oldest annual Indian fair in existence. It features an Indian market, traditional song and dance, barbecue, food booths, pow-wow and rodeo. The fair is held on the Navajo Reservation.

*Easy Chorizo Sausage

This traditional spicy, pork sausage is used in casseroles, stews, soups and enchilada and huevos dishes. This homemade version is much better than prepared chorizos sold in stores.

4 to 6 New Mexico dried red chiles
2 to 3 cloves garlic, minced
1 teaspoon ground cumin
¾ teaspoon salt
1 pound ground pork
1 pound ground beef
¼ cup tequila

 Mix all ingredients in large bowl. Use hands to blend the 2 meats and seasonings. When mixture is the same color throughout, roll into 2 big balls, cover and chill several hours or overnight. Freeze any unused chorizo.

Mission Pork Chops and Gravy

6 to 8 (½-inch) thick pork chops
1 (7 ounce) can chopped green chiles
8 to 10 new potatoes, unpeeled, quartered
2 (10 ounce) cans cream of mushroom soup with roasted garlic

 Preheat oven to 350°.

 Sprinkle salt and pepper on pork chops. In skillet, brown pork chops in a little oil and place in greased 9 x 13-inch baking dish. Place green chiles and potatoes around and over pork chops.

 In saucepan, heat mushroom soup with ½ cup water and pour over chops and potatoes. Cover and cook for 1 hour.

Sunday Ranch Pork Chops

6 (¾-inch) boneless pork chops
1 (1.3 ounce) packet ranch dressing mix
½ teaspoon salt
2 to 3 New Mexico red chiles, seeded, chopped
2 (15 ounce) cans new potatoes, drained, quartered
1 (10 ounce) can French onion soup

❥ Sprinkle pork chops with ranch dressing mix and salt; brown in a little oil in large skillet with lid.

❥ Place chiles and potatoes around and over pork chops. Pour onion soup over pork chops and potatoes. Cover and cook on low for 45 minutes.

Roasted Red Pepper Tenderloin

2 (1 pound) pork tenderloins
1 (1.3 ounce) envelope ranch dressing mix
2 red bell peppers, roasted, chopped
2 New Mexico green chiles, roasted, seeded, chopped
2 jalapenos, seeded, chopped
1 (8 ounce) carton sour cream

❥ In large skillet, brown both tenderloins and place in 6-quart oblong slow cooker.

❥ Combine ranch dressing mix, red bell peppers, green chiles and jalapenos and ½ cup water and spoon over pork tenderloins. Cover and cook on LOW for 4 to 5 hours.

❥ When ready to serve, remove tenderloins from slow cooker. Stir sour cream into sauce in slow cooker. Serve over tenderloin slices.

Tombstone Smothered Pork Chops

6 to 8 lean-cut pork chops
Salt and pepper
2 tablespoons oil
¾ cup uncooked rice
1 (14 ounce) can tomato sauce
1¾ cups water
1 (1 ounce) package taco seasoning mix
1 (8 ounce) package shredded cheddar cheese

 Preheat oven to 350°.

 Sprinkle pork chops with salt and pepper. In skillet, brown pork chops in oil and place in greased 9 x 13-inch baking dish.

 In separate bowl combine rice, tomato sauce, water, taco seasoning and garlic salt and pour over pork chops.

 Cover with foil and bake 1 hour. Uncover and top with cheese and bake 10 minutes more.

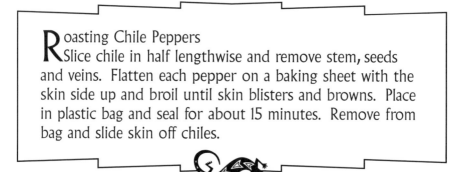

Roasting Chile Peppers
Slice chile in half lengthwise and remove stem, seeds and veins. Flatten each pepper on a baking sheet with the skin side up and broil until skin blisters and browns. Place in plastic bag and seal for about 15 minutes. Remove from bag and slide skin off chiles.

Grilled Pork Tenderloin With Green Chile Rajas

Rajas are fresh green chiles, roasted and cut in strips. The flavor of the pork works well with the rajas.

2 New Mexico green chiles, roasted, peeled, seeded
Salt and pepper
2 cloves garlic, minced
1 pork tenderloin
Seasoned salt
Cracked black pepper

Slice chiles in ¼-inch strips. Season with salt, pepper and garlic and chill for several hours.

Season pork tenderloin with seasoned salt and black pepper and grill just until pink is gone in center. Warm chiles on grill and serve over tenderloin.

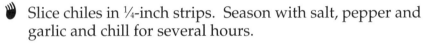

The Old West is alive and well in Tombstone, Arizona, designated a National Historic Landmark in 1962. Ed Schieffelin who prospected for gold on Apache land founded it. He was told, "all you'll find out there is your tombstone". In 1877 he discovered a mountain of silver and the town became the biggest, wildest town west of St. Louis. It is the scene of the "Gunfight at the OK Corral" and reenactments are held every day at 2:00 pm. In Boothill Cemetery the marker for George Johnson, hanged by mistake, reads "He was right, we was wrong, but we strung him up and now he's gone."

Tenderfoot Pork Tenderloin

2 (1 pound) pork tenderloins

SAUCE:
¼ cup oil
1 cup orange juice
2 tablespoons soy sauce
1 (7 ounce) can green Mexican salsa
⅓ cup white wine
2 tablespoons sugar
⅔ cup apricot preserves

❦ Preheat oven to 325°. Place tenderloins in greased 7 x11-inch baking dish. In bowl, combine all sauce ingredients and mix well. Spoon half mixture over tenderloins. Cover and bake for 1 hour.

❦ Remove cover; pour remaining sauce over tenderloins and bake another 35 to 40 minutes. Slice tenderloins diagonally (for larger slices) and spoon sauce over each serving.

The capsaicin in chiles is the heat-producing element found in the veins and oil in chile peppers. Because the seeds are next to the veins, they too contain much of the capsaicin. To remove veins and seeds in chiles will reduce the heat by about 50%. Always wear rubber gloves when handling chiles.

*Carne Adovado, New Mexico-Style

Carne Adovado is a traditional dish served as a main course, stuffed in tortillas or used in enchiladas. It is one of the basic dishes in Southwestern cooking.

2 tablespoons bacon drippings or shortening
2 tablespoons flour
8 to 12 New Mexico dried red chiles
3 cloves garlic, minced
2 teaspoons whole leaf oregano, crushed
3 cups water
2 to 2½ pounds lean pork, sliced in strips

꙰ Heat bacon drippings or shortening over medium heat and spinkle flour over top. Stir constantly while adding chiles, garlic and oregano. (Do not burn flour.)

꙰ Slowly pour water into skillet while stirring. Simmer until sauce thickens slightly. Place pork in greased, 9 x 13-inch baking dish and pour sauce over top. Cover with foil or lid and marinate in refrigerator overnight.

꙰ Preheat oven to 300°. Bake pork in sauce for about 2 hours or until pork falls apart. Serve with flour tortillas.

The Santa Fe Opera is one the most famous and best summer opera companies in the U.S. It runs from June through August in an open-air amphitheater.

✷Classic Hot Tamales

Tamales are a Mexican tradition at Christmas and holidays. The whole family participates in their preparation and it is a fun, family celebration.

2 pounds corn husks
16 New Mexico dried red chiles
1 onion, chopped
3 cloves garlic, minced
1 tablespoon lard or shortening
*2 cups meat stock, divided
4 tablespoons salt, divided
3 pounds boneless pork, beef or chicken with stock, cooked, shredded
1 pound lard (no substitute)
3 pounds masa harina
3 tablespoons baking powder

*(*Use meat stock from cooked pork, beef or chicken.)*

💧 Wipe silks from corn husks, wash in warm water and dry.

💧 Wash dried chiles, remove seeds and stems. Bring to boil in water and simmer about 10 minutes. Pour water and chiles into blender and process. Strain into large bowl to remove pieces of skin.

💧 Saute onions, garlic and oregano in lard or shortening. Add 2 cups chile sauce mixture, 1 cup broth, 2 tablespoons salt and shredded meats and simmer about 15 to 20 minutes. If mixture becomes too thick, add more broth.

💧 Whip melted lard fluffy. Add masa, remaining salt and baking powder. Whip until mixture is light and fluffy. (Masa should float when dropped into glass of cold water.)

💧 Add remaining 2 cups chile sauce and 2 cups broth and mix well. Masa should be stirring consistency. Add broth if needed.

(Continued on next page.)

(Continued)

⚱ Place heaping spoonful masa in middle of husk and spread close to top, out to edges and about 1½ inches from bottom. Place 2 spoonfuls filling on top of masa and spread top to bottom.

⚱ Roll husk and fold bottom 1½ inches up. Place in baking dish with fold on bottom. Repeat process until all filling is used. Stack tamales upright in slow cooker with folded end down. Pour a little water in bottom, cover and steam on HIGH for 3 to 4 hours or until tamales unroll from husks. Makes about 36 tamales.

TAMALE TIPS

⚱ Fillings for tamales may be made in advance and chilled. Save meat stock to use in tamales.

⚱ One pound of meat and one pound of masa will make about 12 tamales.

⚱ Beef, chicken and pork may be used as fillings or a combination of fillings.

⚱ Corn husks, red chile sauce and masa harina may be purchased at the grocery store. Homemade red chile sauce is far superior to prepared chile sauces.

⚱ The cut end of the corn husk is used for the top of the tamale and the pointed end is used as the bottom and is the part that is folded upwards.

Corn husks are used fresh or dried (with the silks removed) for vegetable dishes and tamales. Husks are soaked in water to make them pliable. Fresh husks are shaped into boats by tying the ends with twine to form the shape of boats. Sauteed vegetables are placed inside. Dried husks are used to encase tamales and are rolled and folded.

*Hot-to-Trot Tamale Pie

2 pounds lean pork
7 cups water, divided
3 tablespoons flour
5 tablespoons plus 2 teaspoons red chile powder
1 tablespoon salt
½ teaspoon oregano
½ teaspoon garlic powder
2 cups yellow cornmeal
1 teaspoon salt

- Preheat oven to 350°.

- Boil pork in 1 cup water until pork cooks. Remove pork from water, but reserve liquid. Cool and chop pork and set aside.

- In large skillet pour 1 tablespoon reserved pork stock and flour and stir until flour is smooth and browns slightly.

- Pour remaining reserved pork stock, 5 tablespoons red chile powder, salt, oregano and garlic powder into skillet and cook over low heat until seasonings dissolve. Add chopped pork to skillet, simmer and stir until mixture thickens.

- Dissolve cornmeal in 2 cups cold water and stir in remaining red chile powder and salt. Pour cornmeal mixture into 4 cups boiling water and stir constantly until mixture thickens.

- Pour half of thick cornmeal mixture into prepared casserole dish. Spoon pork mixture on top of cornmeal mixture and cover with remaining cornmeal mixture. Bake for 1 hour to 1 hour 30 minutes or until pie is firm and top browns.

Southwest-Seasoned Pork

2 pounds boneless pork shoulder
½ cup flour
⅓ cup oil
1 onion, finely chopped
3 slices bacon, chopped
½ cup water
½ cup orange juice
2 tablespoons lime juice
3 teaspoons instant, dry chicken bouillon
2 teaspoons cumin
1 teaspoon oregano
1 teaspoon cilantro
⅛ teaspoon cayenne pepper
1 teaspoon salt
1 teaspoon black pepper
4 tomatoes, peeled, chopped
½ cup sour cream
Cooked rice

Cut pork into bite-size pieces, coat with flour and brown in oil in large skillet. Remove pork with slotted spoon and set aside.

In same skillet, cook and stir onion and bacon until bacon is crisp. Stir in pork and remaining ingredients except sour cream and cooked rice.

Heat to boiling and reduce heat. Cover and simmer until pork is done about 45 minutes. Stir in sour cream and serve over hot rice.

Apple-Glazed Pork Roast

1 (12 ounce) jar apple jelly
4 teaspoons dijon mustard
3 teaspoons lemon juice, divided
Black pepper
¼ teaspoon garlic powder
1 (3 to 4 pound) pork loin roast
3 tablespoons brandy

 Preheat oven to 350°.

 In small saucepan, melt jelly over low heat. Stir in mustard and 1 teaspoon lemon juice and set aside. Rub roast with black pepper and garlic powder.

 Place on rack in foil-lined shallow roasting pan and bake for about 45 minutes. Remove from oven, brush with jelly mixture and bake for 20 minutes.

 Brush once more with jelly mixture, turn oven to 325° and bake for additional 1 hour. Remove roast to warm platter.

 Scrape any browned drippings into remaining jelly mixture. Add 2 teaspoons lemon juice and brandy to mixture, bring to boil and turn heat off.

 To serve, sauce plate and place thin slices of roast on top or serve roast on platter with sauce.

A t 7,000 feet above sea level, Santa Fe is the highest state capital.

PORK

Chief Black Beans and Ham

2 (15 ounce) cans black beans, rinsed, drained
1 (8 ounce) can shoepeg corn, drained
3½ cups smoked ham, cubed
6 green onions with tops, chopped
2 tomatoes, peeled, chopped, drained
2 jalapeno peppers, seeded, minced
1 sweet red bell pepper, chopped
½ green bell pepper, chopped
⅓ cup fresh chopped cilantro

DRESSING:
½ cup red wine vinegar
2 tablespoons dijon mustard
2 tablespoons honey
1 teaspoon salt
2 cloves garlic, minced
½ teaspoon dried thyme
¼ cup olive oil
¼ cup vegetable oil

👋 Combine and mix beans, corn, ham, onions, tomatoes, jalapenos and bell peppers and set aside.

👋 In small bowl, combine all dressing ingredients and mix well. Pour dressing over beans and ham mixture and toss. Add cilantro and toss again. Chill, covered, for several hours before serving.

Grilled Swordfish Steaks With Avocado Salsa

4 fresh green onions with tops, finely diced
8 to 10 grape tomatoes, quartered
2 whole, pickled jalapenos, seeded, chopped
¼ cup fresh lime juice
¼ cup snipped fresh cilantro
¾ teaspoon salt
Cracked black pepper
4 swordfish steaks
3 ripe avocados

🖐 Mix all ingredients except swordfish and avocado in medium bowl and chill.

🖐 Grill swordfish steaks on each side about 3 minutes or until grill marks show. Check center of steaks and remove from grill when almost white. Do not overcook and dry out fish.

🖐 Peel avocados, chop and stir into salsa. Serve swordfish steak and top with avocado salsa.

Reports of the medicinal benefits of red chile were recorded as early as the 1700's. People rubbed the chile powder on their gums to relieve the pain of toothaches. Chile powder was also used as a meat preservative.

New Mexico Red Snapper

1 (8 ounce) can tomato sauce
1 (4 ounce) can chopped green chiles
1 clove garlic, minced
1 pound red snapper fillets

- In small bowl, mix tomato sauce, green chiles and garlic. Put snapper fillets on microwave-safe dish and brush tomato sauce mixture evenly over red snapper.

- Cover with plastic wrap. Microwave on HIGH about 3 minutes, rotate dish and microwave 2 minutes.

- Check snapper to see if it flakes easily. If not, microwave another 2 minutes and check to see if meat is flaky.

Pan-Seared Shrimp Ancho

3 to 4 ancho chiles
6 to 8 cloves garlic, minced
1½ cups extra virgin olive oil
2 pounds fresh shrimp, shelled, veined
Salt and cracked black pepper

- Clean ancho chiles well with dry cloth, heat for several minutes in lightly oiled skillet and soak in hot water for about 30 minutes.

- Dry chiles, remove stems and seeds and slice in long, thin strips. Place in large cast-iron or heavy skillet with garlic and about ¼ to ½ cup hot oil. Cook about 1 to 2 minutes.

- Add shrimp and cook until they turn pink. Season with salt and pepper and serve over rice or with bread and salad.

Grilled Tuna
With Roasted Chile Salsa

4 to 5 poblano chiles
3 mild jalapeno peppers
2 red bell peppers
2 yellow bell peppers
1 large sweet onion, minced
4 to 5 cloves garlic, minced
¼ cup extra virgin olive oil
¼ cup fresh lime juice
¼ cup snipped cilantro or oregano
Salt and cracked black pepper
4 to 6 tuna steaks

To roast poblano chiles, hold them over open-flame gas burner with long metal fork or broil in oven until outside turns dark brown on all sides. (Be careful not to burn holes through skin.) Place chiles in plastic bag, seal and allow to sweat for about 15 to 20 minutes so skin will slide off easily. Remove skins and slice through length of chile on one side. Remove seeds, but leave veins intact.

Remove seeds and veins from jalapenos and bell peppers. Chop or mince peppers and mix with all remaining ingredients except fish.

Cook tuna steaks on each side about 3 minutes or until grill marks show. Check center of steaks and remove from grill just when pink in center is almost gone. Do not overcook and dry out fish.

Serve hot with Roasted Chile Salsa on top.

*Fish Tacos

¾ pound boned white fish
2 tablespoons lime juice
1 teaspoon white pepper
6 to 8 corn tortillas
Shredded lettuce
Finely chopped tomatoes
Salsa

Season fish with lime juice and white pepper. In skillet with a little oil, cook fish about 2 minutes on each side until fish flakes easily. Shred each piece of fish and set aside.

Wrap about 5 tortillas in slightly damp paper towel and heat tortillas in microwave for 45 seconds.

When ready to serve, place about 2 tablespoons shredded fish, lettuce and tomatoes in tortilla and fold over. Serve with salsa.

*Fish Tacos With Cilantro Pesto

CILANTRO PESTO:
1 cup packed cilantro leaves
2 teaspoons lime juice
1 teaspoon minced garlic
¼ cup parmesan cheese
⅓ cup olive oil

Prepare fish with same ingredients and in same manner as Fish Tacos above. Mix all ingredients for Cilantro Pesto and serve with Fish Tacos.

Top-Shelf Tequila Shrimp

1½ pounds medium shrimp, shelled, veined
¼ cup (½ stick) butter
2 tablespoons olive oil
2 garlic cloves, minced
3 tablespoons tequila
1½ tablespoons lime juice
½ teaspoon salt
½ teaspoon chile powder
4 tablespoons coarsely chopped fresh cilantro
Hot cooked rice
Lime wedges for garnish

❦ Pat shrimp dry with paper towels. Heat butter and oil in large skillet over medium heat. Add garlic and shrimp and cook about 2 minutes, stirring occasionally.

❦ Stir in tequila, lime juice, salt and chile powder. Cook 2 minutes more or until most liquid evaporates and shrimp are pink and glazed.

❦ Add cilantro and serve over hot cooked rice and garnish with lime wedges.

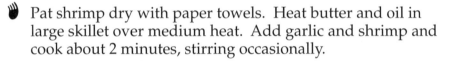

Tequila is a clear liquor made from the century plant or agave cactus that grows in the desert.

Shrimp Cayenne

½ cup (1 stick) butter
2 pounds shrimp, shelled, veined
½ cup green onions with tops, chopped
½ cup chopped celery
½ cup dry white wine
½ teaspoon salt
½ teaspoon pepper
½ teaspoon cayenne
1 tablespoon crab-boil seasoning
½ cup taco sauce
1 tablespoon lemon juice

✹ In large skillet melt butter and saute shrimp, onion and celery until shrimp are pink and onion is translucent.

✹ Add wine, salt, pepper, cayenne, crab-boil, taco sauce and lemon juice and stir well. Cover and simmer for about 5 minutes before serving.

Drying chiles is an excellent way to preserve them. Use only chiles with thin skins and flesh and ones that are ripe, usually reflected by the red color. Bell peppers, for instance, do not dry well. New Mexico, poblano and serrano chiles are excellent varieties to dry. String them together by tying stems together and hang them in a very dry place. Freeze them when they are completely dry and use them whole, crushed, chopped or ground into a fine powder.

Santa Fe Pasta and Shrimp

2 tablespoons butter
1 tablespoon olive oil
½ pound fresh peeled, veined shrimp
½ poblano pepper, seeded, slivered
½ red bell pepper, sliced
¼ red onion, thinly sliced
1 clove garlic, minced
2 tablespoons chopped cilantro leaves
2 tablespoons tequila or gin
½ teaspoon seasoned salt
¼ teaspoon chile powder
½ teaspoon cumin powder
¼ teaspoon black pepper
⅓ cup half-and-half cream
2 cups cooked angel-hair pasta
Grated parmesan cheese

In large skillet, heat butter and oil. Add shrimp and cook about 8 minutes. When shrimp are pink and firm, remove and set aside.

Add peppers, onion, garlic and cilantro and saute until just barely tender. Remove vegetables and set aside.

Add tequila to skillet and swirl it around pan. Add all seasoning and cream. Allow sauce to thicken slightly.

Return shrimp and vegetables to skillet and toss until mixture heats well and coats shrimp with cream. Serve immediately over hot, cooked pasta. Garnish with parmesan cheese.

High Plains Venison Backstrap

Backstrap is the tenderloin of venison and the very best part.

3 to 4 pound venison backstrap
Milk to cover
1½ cups flour
1 teaspoon salt
½ teaspoon black pepper
Oil
Milk or half-and-half

- Place backstrap in bowl and cover with milk. Soak in refrigerator several hours or overnight.

- Remove from milk and cut into ¼-inch slices. In shallow bowl, combine flour, salt and pepper and dredge each backstrap slice in flour mixture.

- Cook on medium heat until slices are light brown.

- For gravy, use 2 tablespoons seasoned flour and brown in skillet with pan drippings.

- Pour in about 2 cups milk or cream, stir constantly and cook until gravy thickens. If gravy is too thick, add a little more milk.

Pickling chiles is one way of preserving them. This method usually calls for preserving chiles in a solution of vinegar, sugar, salt and sometimes garlic, onion, coriander seeds and dill. Other herbs and ingredients may be used also.

Wild Game Stew

In the mountains and the higher elevations of the Southwest, deer, elk, bighorn sheep and bear still roam the land. In the days of Spanish explorers and nomadic and Puebloan Indians, the stew probably had meat from the last kill and roots and nuts found along the trails. This stew has to be much better than anything available in the "old" days.

1 (28 ounce) can Mexican stewed tomatoes
2 (15 ounce) cans beef broth
2 to 3 pounds venison, cubed
Bacon drippings or olive oil
1 (6 ounce) bottle worcestershire sauce
2 to 3 teaspoons paprika
2 teaspoons salt
2 teaspoons black pepper
2 to 3 jalapenos, seeded, chopped
5 to 6 potatoes, chopped
3 to 4 large onions, chopped
1 (16 ounce) bag baby carrots, sliced
3 to 4 ribs celery, chopped

- Pour tomatoes and beef broth into large Dutch oven or large stew pot and turn heat to warm.

- In large skillet brown venison in bacon drippings. Pour venison and pan drippings into stew pot.

- Add worcestershsire sauce, paprika, salt, pepper and jalapenos. Bring stew to boil, reduce heat to low and cook about 2 to 3 hours or until venison is fairly tender.

- Add potatoes, onions and carrots and cook on low heat another 1 to 2 hours. Adjust seasonings to taste as stew cooks.

- Add celery about 15 to 20 minutes before serving to give stew a little crunch.

*Pan-Fried Venison Strips

In the Old West they did not always have eggs or milk, so they fried venison in a heavy cast-iron skillet with just flour, meat, salt and pepper and beef suet for the oil. If they did not have flour, salt and pepper, they just fried the meat in small pieces and they were glad to get it.

1½ pounds venison steak, thinly sliced
1½ cups flour
1 teaspoon salt
1 teaspoon black pepper
1 egg, beaten
¼ cup milk
Oil for frying

Pound steak very thin and cut into long, narrow slices. In shallow bowl, combine flour, salt and black pepper.

In second shallow bowl, combine egg and milk. Dredge steaks in flour mixture, dip in egg mixture and again in flour.

In heavy skillet over medium heat with about ¼ inch oil, fry steak pieces until golden brown. Drain on paper towels.

Lard is traditionally rendered from pork fat and at one time was the only fat available for Southwest cooking. It has a unique, rich flavor that cannot be equaled by vegetable oils or butter. Lard is considered essential for tamales.

Tribal Council Venison Chile

No doubt the Puebloan Indians cooked some kind of meat chile. This recipe has more ingredients than they probably used, but it is still a meat chile. Chase this "Chile Con Carne" with flour tortillas and jalapenos.

¼ cup olive oil
4 onions, minced
2 to 3 pounds venison, cubed
1 pound ground pork sausage or bacon, optional
Salt
Black pepper
3 to 4 cups water, divided
6 to 8 dried New Mexico Red chile peppers, ground
3 to 4 jalapenos, seeded, chopped
2 to 3 cloves garlic, minced
2 teaspoons paprika
2 teaspoons cumin

- In large Dutch oven or heavy roasting pan, brown onions in oil until they are translucent. Add cubed venison, a little at a time, and brown on all sides. Salt and pepper venison as it browns. Add a little oil if needed.

- Pour in 1 to 2 cups water, New Mexico Reds, jalapenos, garlic, paprika and cumin and stir well. Cook over high heat, uncovered, for about 10 minutes, then reduce heat to low and cook 2 to 3 hours. (Add more water if needed for consistency desired. Adjust seasonings if water is added.)

- Reduce heat to simmer and cook another 1 to 2 hours.

TIP: Taste the chili as it cooks to adjust seasonings and liquid.

Fried Game Birds

10 to 12 quail or dove
1 (6 ounce) can frozen orange juice concentrate, thawed
1 teaspoon lemon juice
½ teaspoon salt
1 to 2 cups biscuit mix
Oil

🖐 In large shallow bowl, combine orange juice concentrate, lemon juice and salt. Place birds in bowl, add enough water to cover birds and marinate for 2 to 3 hours.

🖐 Pour biscuit mix in shallow bowl and dredge birds in biscuit mix to cover well. Fry birds in heated, deep-fat fryer until light brown. Drain on paper towels and serve hot.

Wild Turkey Breasts

This is a real delicacy for today's hunters and it was probably just as special to the Indians and cowboys of the Southwest.

Dressed wild turkey breasts
Salt
Freshly ground black pepper
Flour
Milk
Cooking oil

🖐 Slice turkey breasts in thin strips across the grain. Season with salt and black pepper generously. Dip both sides in flour, dip in milk and again in flour.

🖐 Place in large, heavy skillet with hot oil and cook on both sides until golden brown. Do not overcook. Drain on paper towels and serve immediately.

*Grilled Jalapeno-Stuffed Doves

MARINADE:
¾ cup tarragon vinegar
¼ cup worcestershire sauce
¼ cup sugar
2 teaspoons garlic powder
1 teaspoon seasoned salt
¼ teaspoon ground coriander
1 cup oil

8 to 10 doves, cleaned
5 to 6 jalapenos, seeded, halved
1 (1 pound) package Colby cheese
8 to 10 slices bacon

- In large glass bowl or baking dish, mix all marinade ingredients and set aside.

- Slice breasts off dove and drop in marinade. Cover bowl, chill and marinate at least 24 hours. Mix marinade and dove several times to blend ingredients.

- Remove dove breasts from marinade and discard marinade. Drain breasts and make a sandwich using one breast, one jalapeno half, one slice cheese and one breast together. Tie together with one slice bacon and secure with toothpick.

- Place on grill over medium fire and cook until bacon is crispy. Turn several times while grilling.

Venison Jerky

2 tablespoons vinegar
2 tablespoons steak sauce
1 teaspoon liquid smoke
1 teaspoon garlic salt
½ teaspoon black pepper
1 to 3 jalapenos, seeded, chopped
1 onion, minced
2 to 3 pounds venison

- In large bowl, mix vinegar, steak sauce, liquid smoke, garlic salt and black pepper and whisk thoroughly. Add jalapenos and onion to marinade and set aside.

- Cut venison into strips about ¼ inch thick and about 1 inch wide.

- Add venison to marinade and mix well. Make sure all venison is covered with marinade. Seal and store in refrigerator for 24 hours.

- Remove from refrigerator, drain venison strips and place on baking sheet with space in between all pieces.

- Bake in oven at 200° for about 5 hours. Turn once or twice while cooking.

Dried chiles are usually milder than the fresh ones of the same variety.

Fried Rattlesnake

In the Sonoran, Chihuahuan, Mojave and Great Basin Deserts of the Southwest, rattlesnakes are under every rock. There's no doubt that native Indians and lots of cowboys ate rattlesnake.

Rattlesnake, cleaned, skinned
Salt
Freshly ground black pepper
Cornmeal or masa harina
Buttermilk
Cooking oil

- Slice rattlesnake in medallions about ½ to ¾ inch thick. Season with salt and black pepper generously. Dip both sides in cornmeal, dip in buttermilk and again in flour.

- Place in large, heavy skillet with hot oil and cook on both sides until golden brown. Do not overcook. Drain on paper towels and serve immediately.

TIP: To make buttermilk, mix 1 cup milk with 2 tablespoons lemon juice or vinegar and let milk rest for about 10 minutes.

Desert flora and fauna throughout the Southwest provided food for native Indians. More than 100 species of cactus including prickly pear and the giant saguaro, yucca plants, agave, sagebrush, ponderosa pine and in the higher elevations the Douglas fir, aspen and other conifers flourished and continue to grow today. Chaparral, rattlesnakes, javelina, the desert tortoise, jackrabbits, mountain lions, bear, bighorn sheep, elk and deer were abundant in a wild land. Many are protected from extinction today.

DESSERTS

Caballero Cookies

2 cups flour
1 teaspoon baking soda
½ teaspoon baking powder
½ teaspoon salt
1 cup (2 sticks) butter
1 cup sugar
1 cup packed brown sugar
2 eggs
1 teaspoon vanilla
2 cups quick-cooking oats
1 (6 ounce) package chocolate chips
1 cup chopped pecans

● Preheat oven to 350°.

● Sift flour, baking soda, baking powder and salt and set aside.

● Cream butter, sugars, eggs and vanilla until fluffy. Add flour mixture and mix well. Add oats, chocolate chips and pecans and mix well.

● Drop by teaspoon onto greased cookie sheet and bake for about 15 minutes. For a fun cookie, make large cookies using ¼ cup cookie dough. Bake 2 or 3 minutes longer.

Toasting Chile Peppers
Place clean, dried chiles on baking pan and bake in oven at 250° until chiles are lightly toasted, but not burned. Remove stems and seeds and grind in food processor. Store in an airtight container.

Snow-Covered Cookies

½ cup (1 stick) butter, softened
1¼ cups powdered sugar, divided
1 teaspoon vanilla
1 cup flour
1 cup finely chopped pine nuts
½ teaspoon anise seed, crushed
Pinch of salt

 Preheat oven to 275°.

 In mixing bowl, combine butter, ½ cup powdered sugar and vanilla and beat until creamy. Stir in flour, nuts, anise seed and salt.

 Shape dough in 1-inch balls and place on ungreased baking sheet. Bake for 30 to 35 minutes or until cookies are light brown. Roll warm cookies in remaining powdered sugar, cool and roll in sugar again.

The planet Pluto was discovered by astronomer, Clyde Tombaugh, at the Lowell Observatory in Flagstaff, Arizona in 1930. The Observatory won its international reputation with its documented evidence of the expanding universe.

✴Biscochitos

Biscochitos are traditional Mexican cookies usually served at holidays with hot chocolate.

3 cups flour
1½ teaspoons anise seed
1½ teaspoons baking powder
½ teaspoon salt
1 cup shortening
½ teaspoon vanilla
1½ cups sugar
2 eggs
¼ cup orange juice
2 teaspoons cinnamon
½ cup sugar

- Preheat oven to 350°.

- Combine flour, anise seed, baking powder and salt in bowl and set aside.

- Beat shortening and vanilla with electric mixer until creamy, add sugar and beat until fluffy. Blend in eggs and beat again.

- Gradually add flour mixture alternately with orange juice and mix well after each addition. Divide dough in half and roll out 1 portion at a time on lightly floured board to ¼-inch thickness.

- Cut out cookies with fancy cookie cutters. As you cut cookies, add scraps to remaining dough. If dough becomes too sticky to handle, chill briefly.

- Mix cinnamon and sugar and sprinkle over cookies. Bake for 8 to 10 minutes or until edges begin to brown. Cool on rack.

Lazy Biscochitos

1 cup shortening
2 cups flour
½ cup powdered sugar
2 teaspoons anise seed
⅓ cup sugar
1 teaspoon cinnamon

 Preheat oven to 350°.

 Mix shortening, flour, powdered sugar and anise. Press dough into 9 x 9-inch baking pan and pierce dough with fork about every 1 inch.

 Mix sugar and cinnamon and sprinkle over top of dough. Bake for 20 to 25 minutes and cut into small squares.

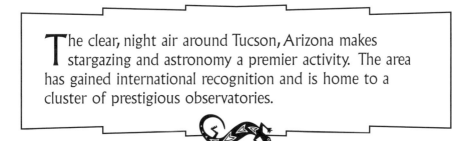

The clear, night air around Tucson, Arizona makes stargazing and astronomy a premier activity. The area has gained international recognition and is home to a cluster of prestigious observatories.

Sierra Nuggets

1 cup (2 sticks) butter
1 cup packed brown sugar
1½ cups white sugar
1 tablespoon milk
2 teaspoons vanilla
2 eggs
1 cup crushed flake cereal
3 cups oatmeal
1½ cups flour
1¼ teaspoons baking soda
1 teaspoon salt
2 teaspoons cinnamon
¼ teaspoon nutmeg
½ cup flaked coconut
2 cups chocolate chips
1 cup chopped walnuts or pecans

● Preheat oven to 350°.

● In large mixing bowl, cream butter and sugars and beat in milk, vanilla and eggs. Stir in flake cereal and oatmeal.

● Sift flour, baking soda, salt and seasonings. Gradually add to cookie mixture. Stir in coconut, chocolate chips and nuts. Drop by teaspoon on cookie sheet and bake for 10 to 15 minutes.

The Sandia Peak Tramway outside of Albuquerque is the longest aerial tramway in the world. On a clear day you can see half of New Mexico from the top of the 10,378-foot high Sandia Peak.

274

Santa Fe Mocha Balls

1 cup butter
½ cup sugar
2 teaspoons vanilla
1¾ cups flour
¼ cup cocoa
1 tablespoon instant coffee granules
1¼ teaspoons salt
1 cup chopped nuts
½ cup chopped maraschino cherries, drained
Powdered sugar

W Cream butter, sugar and vanilla in large bowl. In separate bowl mix flour, cocoa, instant coffee and salt. Gradually pour in dry ingredients with sugar and mix well.

W Stir in nuts and cherries and shape into large ball. Chill for 1 to 2 hours before baking.

W Preheat oven to 350°. Form into 1-inch balls and place on cookie sheet. Bake for about 15 to 20 minutes or until cookies are light brown.

W Dust with powdered sugar while cookies are hot.

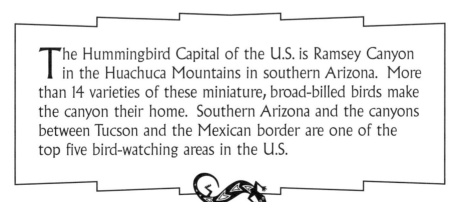

The Hummingbird Capital of the U.S. is Ramsey Canyon in the Huachuca Mountains in southern Arizona. More than 14 varieties of these miniature, broad-billed birds make the canyon their home. Southern Arizona and the canyons between Tucson and the Mexican border are one of the top five bird-watching areas in the U.S.

Ranch Spice Cake

2½ cups flour
1 teaspoon baking powder
1 teaspoon cinnamon
½ teaspoon salt
½ teaspoon allspice
½ teaspoon ginger
½ teaspoon nutmeg
½ cup (1 stick) butter, softened
½ cup sugar
1½ cups packed brown sugar
2 eggs
1 teaspoon vanilla
1 teaspoon baking soda
1¼ cups buttermilk
1 (16 ounce) can caramel frosting
¾ cup chopped pecans

 Preheat oven to 350°.

 Grease 9 x 13-inch baking pan and set aside. Sift flour, baking powder, cinnamon, salt, allspice, ginger and nutmeg.

 In mixing bowl, beat butter, sugars, eggs and vanilla until fluffy. Dissolve baking soda in buttermilk. Beat in half flour mixture, add buttermilk and beat.

 Add remaining flour and beat. Pour into prepared pan. Bake for 45 minutes, remove from oven and cool.

 Spread frosting over cake and sprinkle chopped pecans over top.

Kahlua Cake

1 (18 ounce) chocolate cake mix
¾ cup oil
1 (3 ounce) box instant chocolate pudding
4 eggs
½ cup strong, brewed coffee
¾ cup kahlua

FROSTING:
2½ cups powdered sugar
Kahlua
Chocolate curls

W Preheat oven to 350°.

W In mixing bowl, combine cake mix, oil, chocolate pudding, eggs, coffee and kahlua and beat about 5 minutes.

W Pour into greased, floured 9 x 13-inch baking pan and bake for 40 to 45 minutes.

W When toothpick inserted in center comes out clean, remove from oven and cool. Mix powdered sugar with enough kahlua to make frosting spreading consistency.

W Frost cake and sprinkle chocolate curls on top.

Tucson is Arizona's second largest city and is located in a basin surrounded by five mountain ranges and the Sonoran Desert.

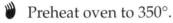

Southwest Chocolate Cake

2 cups sugar
2 cups flour
½ cup (1 stick) butter
½ cup oil
4 heaping tablespoons cocoa
1 cup water
½ cup buttermilk
2 eggs, beaten
1 teaspoon baking soda
1 teaspoon cinnamon
1 teaspoon vanilla
½ teaspoon salt

FROSTING:
½ cup (1 stick) butter, melted
4 tablespoons cocoa
6 tablespoons milk
1 (1 pound) powdered sugar
1 teaspoon vanilla
1 cup chopped pecans
1 (7 ounce) can flaked coconut

 Preheat oven to 350°.

 Blend flour and sugar. In saucepan, bring butter, oil, cocoa and water to a boil, pour over flour and sugar mixture and beat well.

 Add buttermilk, eggs, baking soda, cinnamon, vanilla and salt and mix well. Pour into greased, floured 9 x 13-inch pan and bake for 40 to 45 minutes.

 About 5 minutes before cake is done combine butter, cocoa, milk, powdered sugar and vanilla and mix well. Add pecans and coconut and mix. Spread on hot cake.

Coffee-Rum Cake

1 cup (2 sticks) butter, softened
2 cups sugar
⅔ cup packed brown sugar
4 eggs
3 cups flour
1 teaspoon baking powder
½ teaspoon salt
¼ cup rum
1 cup brewed coffee, cooled

COFFEE-RUM SAUCE:
2 cups sugar
1 cup packed brown sugar
½ cup brewed coffee
¼ cup light corn syrup
½ cup rum

 Preheat oven to 325°.

 Combine and cream butter and sugars in mixing bowl until fluffy. Add eggs, one at a time, and beat well.

Combine flour, baking powder and salt. Stir in rum and coffee. Fold flour mixture into creamed mixture alternately with coffee and rum.

Pour into greased, floured tube or bundt pan and bake for 1 hour 30 minutes or until toothpick comes out clean. Cool about 15 minutes and invert onto cake plate.

For sauce, bring sugars, coffee and syrup to boil for about 2 minutes. Remove from heat and stir in rum. Pour sauce over slices of cake when serving.

Chocolate-Kahlua Cake

3 eggs, separated
1¼ cups sugar, divided
½ cup (1 stick) butter, softened
1 cup packed light brown sugar
2¼ cups flour
½ cup cocoa
1½ teaspoons baking soda
⅔ cup strong cold coffee
⅔ cup kahlua

FROSTING:
1 cup powdered sugar
2 tablespoons cocoa
2 to 3 tablespoons kahlua

 Preheat oven to 350°.

 Beat egg whites until frothy, pour in ¾ cup sugar and beat until stiff peaks form. Set aside. Cream butter, brown sugar and ½ cup sugar until fluffy. Beat in egg yolks one at a time.

 Sift together flour, cocoa and baking soda. Add to creamed mixture alternately with coffee and kahlua and blend well. Fold egg whites into batter.

 Pour into greased, floured bundt pan and bake for 55 to 60 minutes. Test with toothpick for doneness.

 Cool for about 10 to 15 minutes before removing cake from pan. Cool completely before frosting.

 For frosting, blend powdered sugar, cocoa and kahlua, drizzle over top and let some drip down sides of cake.

Terrific Pecan Pie

¾ cup sugar
2 tablespoons flour
¼ teaspoon salt
3 eggs, slightly beaten
1 cup dark corn syrup
1 (5 ounce) can evaporated milk
2 tablespoons butter, melted
1 teaspoon vanilla
1 cup pecans
1 (9 inch) unbaked pie crust

 Preheat oven to 350°.

 In bowl, combine sugar, flour and salt. Stir in eggs, corn syrup, evaporated milk, butter, vanilla and pecans and mix well. Pour into unbaked pie crust.

 Place a 1-inch strip of foil around edges of crust to keep crust from browning too much. Bake for 50 to 60 minutes or until center is set.

Arizona received its nickname, the "Copper State", early in the 20th century when gold, silver and minerals were discovered and the influx of miners turned it into a booming area.

Strawberry-Margarita Pie

¼ cup frozen pink lemonade concentrate, thawed
2 tablespoons tequila
2 tablespoons triple sec
1 teaspoon grated lime peel
1 pint fresh strawberries, sliced
1 quart strawberry ice cream, softened
1 (9 inch) graham cracker pie crust, chilled
Strawberries

🖐 In large mixing bowl, combine and mix lemonade, tequila, triple sec, lime peel and strawberries. Fold in softened ice cream. Work quickly so ice cream will not melt completely.

🖐 Spoon mixture into chilled crust and freeze. Take out of freezer about 10 minutes before serving to slice. Garnish with strawberries.

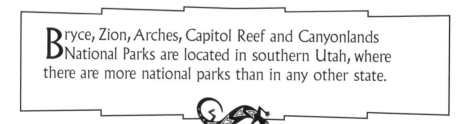

Bryce, Zion, Arches, Capitol Reef and Canyonlands National Parks are located in southern Utah, where there are more national parks than in any other state.

*Frozen Margarita Pie

½ cup (1 stick) butter
1½ cups pretzels, crushed
2 tablespoons sugar
1 (14 ounce) can sweetened condensed milk
¼ cup lime juice
1½ ounces triple sec
1½ ounces tequila
1 (8 ounce) carton whipping cream, whipped
Lime slices for garnish

Combine butter, pretzels and sugar in pie plate, press down to form crust and freeze.

In mixing bowl, combine sweetened condensed milk and lime juice. Fold in triple sec, tequila and whipped cream and freeze overnight.

Take of freezer about 10 minutes before serving to slice.

World famous artist, Georgia O'Keefe was a New Mexico resident for many years and was greatly affected by the vibrant colors of nature all around her. From her summer home for more than 35 years in the small town of Abiquiu, O'Keefe painted some of her most famous work. The last 10 years of her life, O'Keefe lived in Santa Fe and enjoyed brillant, high-altitude sunlight with streaks of yellows, oranges and violets and shadows falling on rich earth tones against a backdrop of the Sangre de Cristo and Jemez mountains. The Georgia O'Keefe Museum in Santa Fe houses more than 100 paintings and small sculptures by New Mexico's most celebrated artist.

*Lime-Margarita Pie

1 (14 ounce) can sweetened condensed milk
2 egg yolks
½ cup sugar
⅓ cup fresh lime juice
1½ ounces tequila
1 ounce cointreau or triple sec
2 egg whites
1 (9 inch) graham cracker crust
½ cup whipping cream, whipped
¼ cup sugar
Lime slices

 Preheat oven to 350°.

 In medium mixing bowl, combine sweetened condensed milk, egg yolks, sugar, lime juice, tequila and cointreau or triple sec and mix well.

 Beat egg whites until slightly stiff and fold them into egg-sugar mixture. Spoon mixture into graham cracker crust. Bake for 25 minutes or until set. Let pie cool.

 Fold sugar into whipped cream and spread over cooled pie. Chill pie several hours before serving. Garnish each piece of pie with thin lime slice.

Kahlua Pie

26 marshmallows
1 (13 ounce) can evaporated milk
1 (.25 ounce) envelope unflavored gelatin
¼ cup cold water
1 (8 ounce) carton whipping cream
½ cup kahlua
1 (9 inch) chocolate cookie pie crust
Chocolate curls

- In saucepan, melt marshmallows in evaporated milk on low heat, stir constantly and do not let milk boil.

- Remove from heat, dissolve gelatin in cold water and add to marshmallow mixture. Chill until mixture thickens slightly.

- Whip cream, fold into marshmallow mixture and mix with kahlua. Pour into pie crust, garnish with chocolate curls and chill overnight.

Kahlua Frappes

¾ cup milk
1 pint coffee ice cream
¾ cup kahlua
Whipped cream
Shaved chocolate

- Pour milk in ice-cube tray and freeze. In blender, combine frozen milk cubes, ice cream and kahlua and blend.

- Pour into parfait glasses and garnish with whipped cream and chocolate shavings.

Strawberry-Margarita Tart

CRUST:
1½ cups finely crushed pretzel crumbs
½ cup (1 stick) butter, melted
⅓ cup sugar

FILLING:
⅓ cup frozen pink lemonade concentrate, thawed
1 tablespoon lime juice
1 (10 ounce) box frozen strawberries, thawed
2 tablespoons triple sec
3 tablespoons tequila
1 quart strawberry ice cream, softened

❦ Combine pretzel crumbs, butter and sugar and mix well. Press mixture in bottom of spring-form pan and chill.

❦ Combine lemonade concentrate, lime juice, strawberries, triple sec and tequila. Work quickly to stir in ice cream and pour into spring-form pan. Cover with plastic wrap and freeze overnight. Garnish with whipped topping and lime slices.

TIP: A food processor crushes pretzels quickly.

The New Mexico Museum of Space History in Alamogordo has the largest collection of artifacts from space explorations in the world.

Margarita Mousse

2 (10 ounce) packages frozen sweetened strawberries,
    thawed
⅓ cup sugar
1 (3 ounce) box strawberry gelatin
½ cup boiling water
2 tablespoons triple sec
3 tablespoons tequila
2 (8 ounce) cartons vanilla yogurt

- Place strawberries and sugar in blender and process until smooth. Place gelatin in bowl, pour boiling water over gelatin and stir until gelatin dissolves.

- Add triple sec, tequila and strawberries and mix well. Cover and chill for about 20 minutes or until mixture begins to thicken.

- Fold in vanilla yogurt and pour into 6 margarita glasses. Cover and chill at least 6 hours or until set.

The Santa Fe National Forest includes more than 230,000 acres of the Pecos Wilderness area. Access to the wilderness is by foot or horse only. The 11,661-foot Elk Mountain is in the wilderness area.

*Mexican Flan

2½ cups sugar, divided
9 eggs
6 cups evaporated milk
2 tablespoons vanilla
½ teaspoon nutmeg
½ teaspoon cinnamon
Whipped cream

 Preheat oven to 350°.

 Caramelize 2 cups sugar in deep saucepan by stirring constantly over low heat. Remove from heat and place into 12, small custard-size cups to coat inside of cups.

 Combine eggs, ½ cup sugar, milk, vanilla, nutmeg and cinnamon and beat well. Pour into custard cups and place cups in 9 x 13-inch baking pan.

 Gently pour in 1-inch water into pan and place on center rack in oven. Bake for about 1 hour or until flan sets. Cool and serve from cup or invert on dessert plate and garnish with nutmeg and cinnamon.

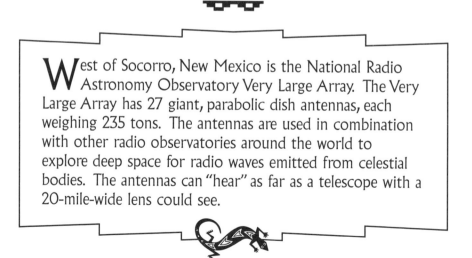

West of Socorro, New Mexico is the National Radio Astronomy Observatory Very Large Array. The Very Large Array has 27 giant, parabolic dish antennas, each weighing 235 tons. The antennas are used in combination with other radio observatories around the world to explore deep space for radio waves emitted from celestial bodies. The antennas can "hear" as far as a telescope with a 20-mile-wide lens could see.

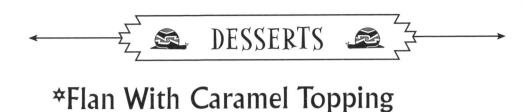

*Flan With Caramel Topping

2⅔ cups sugar, divided
1 tablespoon water
8 eggs
1 teaspoon vanilla
¼ teaspoon salt
½ teaspoon cinnamon
1 quart milk, scalded

 Preheat oven to 350°.

Caramelize 2 cups sugar, add water and cook about
1 minute, stirring constantly. Pour caramel into 12 custard
cups and tilt each cup to coat sides.

Beat eggs lightly and add remaining sugar, vanilla, salt and
cinnamon. Stir in milk and pour into custard cups.

Set cups in pan with about 1 inch hot water and bake for
30 minutes or until a knife near edge comes out clean.
Remove flan from molds to serve.

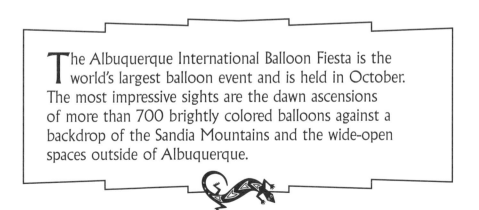

The Albuquerque International Balloon Fiesta is the
world's largest balloon event and is held in October.
The most impressive sights are the dawn ascensions
of more than 700 brightly colored balloons against a
backdrop of the Sandia Mountains and the wide-open
spaces outside of Albuquerque.

Mango-Banana Parfaits

1 (15 ounce) can mangos, drained or 1 pound fresh mangos,
    peeled, sliced
2 very ripe bananas, cut in 1-inch slices
¾ cup sour cream
⅓ cup packed brown sugar
1 tablespoon lime juice
1 (8 ounce) carton whipping cream, whipped
2 cups pecans
1 cup sugar
2 teaspoons cinnamon

❤ Cut mangos in chunks, place mangos, bananas, sour
cream, brown sugar and lime juice in food processor and
puree mixture. Pour mixture in bowl and quickly fold
in whipped cream. Cover and chill at least 3 hours or
overnight.

❤ In large, heavy skillet, combine pecans, sugar and
cinnamon. Cook on medium heat, stirring constantly,
until sugar melts. Continue cooking until sugar is caramel
brown. Pour mixture onto foil-covered baking sheet and
spread out to cool. Coarsely chop.

❤ Do not make parfaits until just before serving. (The
crunchy pecans will get soggy if not served immediately).
To make parfaits in 6 parfait glasses, layer mango-banana
mixture and crunchy pecans twice and end with crunchy
pecans. Serve immediately.

Mexican-Chocolate Ice Cream

3 eggs
1¼ cups sugar
2 quarts half-and-half cream
1 (16 ounce) can chocolate syrup
¾ teaspoon ground cinnamon
1 tablespoon vanilla
¼ teaspoon almond extract

Beat eggs at medium speed in electric mixer. Gradually add sugar and beat until thick. Heat half-and-half in 3-quart saucepan over low heat until hot, but do not boil.

Gradually stir about ¼ hot mixture into eggs and mix well. Add to remaining hot mixture and stir constantly. Cook over low heat, stirring constantly, until mixture thickens slightly.

Remove from heat and stir in chocolate syrup, cinnamon, vanilla and almond extract. Chill in refrigerator for about 1 hour and pour into freezer can of 1-gallon ice cream freezer.

Freeze according to manufacturer's directions.

The word "chocolate" is derived from the Aztec word "xocolatl". The Aztecs were the first to use cocoa beans mixed with spices to create a drink. Mexican hot chocolate is famous around the world, as well as mole, a sauce that uses chocolate and other spices.

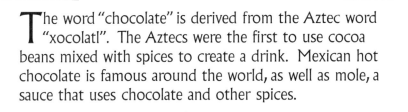

Kahlua-Chocolate Strawberries

1 (6 ounce) package semi-sweet chocolate pieces
½ cup sweetened condensed milk
⅓ cup kahlua
2 pints fresh strawberries

◖ In top of double boiler, melt chocolate over simmering water. Add milk, stir and remove from heat. Add kahlua and stir until it blends well. Cool until it thickens, about 1 hour. Recipe makes about 1 cup sauce.

◖ Use only firm, dry strawberries and hand dip. Chill and serve within several hours. Guests also like to dip their own strawberries.

*Cinnamon Crisps

Flour tortillas
Vegetable oil
Sugar
Ground cinnamon

◖ Cut tortillas into pie shapes and carefully place in large skillet with hot oil. Fry until golden brown, remove from skillet and drain on paper towels. Sprinkle both sides of tortilla wedges heavily with sugar and cinnamon.

The oldest professional rodeo in the world is held annually in Prescott, Arizona during Frontier Days in June.

Bibliography

Barbara C. Jones, *Southwest Ole*, Bonham, Tx. 1993

Dave DeWitt, Nancy Gerlach & Jeff Gerlach, *Too Many Chilies*, Phoenix, Az. 2001

Eve Zibart, *The Ethnic Food Lovers Companion*, Birmingham, Al 2001

Helen Siegel and Karen Gillingham, *The Totally Chile Pepper Cookbook*, Berkely, Ca 1994

Irene Barraza Sanchex & Gloria Sanchez Yund, *Comida Sabrosa*, Albuquerque, NM 2001

Joan Stromquist, Santa Fe, *Light & Spicy Recipes*, Santa Fe, NM 1992

Judy Hille Walker, *Savory Southwest*, Flagstaff, Az, 1990

Judy Walker & Kim MacEachern, *Chips, Dips & Salsas*, Flagstaff, Az. 1999

Judy Walker & Kim MacEachern, *Southwestern Soups, Stews & Skillet Suppers*, Flagstaff, Az 2000

Junior League of El Paso, *Seasoned With Sun*, El Paso, 1989

Karen Adler, *The Best Little Grilling Cookbook*, Berkeley, Ca. 2000

Karen Hursh Graber, *Take This Chile and Stuff It*, Phoenix, Az, 1998

Kathleen Hansel & Audrey Jenkins, *Red Chile Bible*. Santa Fe, NM 1998

Linda Matthie-Jacobs, *Light The Fire*, Calgary, Canada 1959

Lisa Golden Schroeder, *Sizzling Southwestern Cookery*, New York, NY 1990

Lynn Nunsom, *The Tequila Cook Book*, Phoenix, Az. 1993

Mad Coyote Joe, *A Gringo's Guide to Authenic Mexican Cooking*, Flagstaff, Az. 2001

Marcia Keegan, *Southwest Indian Cookbook*, Santa Fe, NM, 1996

Mark Miller, *The Great Chile Book*, Berkeley, Ca. 1991

Richard Harris, *Hidden New Mexico*, Berkely, Ca. 1997

Robert Berkley, *Peppers A Cookbook*, New York, NY 1992

Sandy Szwarc, *Real New Mexico Chile*, Phoenix, Az. 2003

Shayne Fischer, *Wholly Frijoles*, Phoenix, Az. 1994

Susan K. Bollin, *Quick-N-Easy Mexican Recipes*, Phoenix, Az 1993

Symphony Guild Cookbook, *Savoring The Southwest*, Roswell, Nm 1967

The Albuquerque Tribune, *Green Chile Bible*, Santa Fe, NM, 1994

INDEX

INDEX

INDEX

INDEX

INDEX

INDEX

COOKBOOKS PUBLISHED BY COOKBOOK RESOURCES, LLC

The Ultimate Cooking With 4 Ingredients
4 Ingredient Recipes And 30-Minute Meals
Easy Cooking With 5 Ingredients
The Best of Cooking With 3 Ingredients
Easy Gourmet-Style Cooking With 5 Ingredients
Gourmet Cooking With 5 Ingredients
Healthy Cooking With 4 Ingredients
Easy Dessert Cooking With 5 Ingredients
Easy Slow-Cooker Cooking
Quick Fixes With Mixes
Casseroles To The Rescue
Kitchen Keepsakes/More Kitchen Keepsakes
Mother's Recipes
Recipe Keepsakes
Cookie Dough Secrets
Gifts For The Cookie Jar
Brownies In A Jar
101 Brownies
Cookie Jar Magic
Quilters' Cooking Companion
Classic Southern Cooking
Classic Tex-Mex and Texas Cooking
Classic Southwest Cooking
Classic Pennsylvania-Dutch Cooking
The Great Canadian Cookbook
The Best of Lone Star Legacy Cookbook
Lone Star Legacy
Lone Star Legacy II
Cookbook 25 Years
Pass The Plate
Authorized Texas Ranger Cookbook
Texas Longhorn Cookbook
Trophy Hunters' Guide To Cooking
Mealtimes and Memories
Holiday Recipes
Homecoming
Little Taste of Texas
Little Taste of Texas II
Texas Peppers
Southwest Sizzler
Southwest Ole
Class Treats
Leaving Home

cookbook
resources LLC
Bringing Family And Friends To The Table

To Order **Classic Southwest Cooking**:

Please send_____copies @ $19.95 (U.S.) each $_____

Plus postage/handling @ $6.00 each $_____

Texas residents add sales tax @ $1.45 each $_____

Check or Credit Card (Canada-credit card only) **Total** $_____

Charge to my ☐ MasterCard. or ☐ VISA

Account #_____

Expiration Date_____

Signature_____

Mail or Call:
Cookbook Resources
541 Doubletree Dr.
Highland Village, Texas 75077
Toll Free (866) 229-2665
(972) 317-6404 Fax

Name_____

Address_____

City_____State_____Zip_____

Phone (day)_____(night)_____

— —

To Order **Classic Southwest Cooking**:

Please send_____copies @ $19.95 (U.S.) each $_____

Plus postage/handling @ $6.00 each $_____

Texas residents add sales tax @ $1.45 each $_____

Check or Credit Card (Canada-credit card only) **Total** $_____

Charge to my ☐ MasterCard. or ☐ VISA

Account #_____

Expiration Date_____

Signature_____

Mail or Call:
Cookbook Resources
541 Doubletree Dr.
Highland Village, Texas 75077
Toll Free (866) 229-2665
(972) 317-6404 Fax

Name_____

Address_____

City_____State_____Zip_____

Phone (day)_____(night)_____